Aunt up for Perth

Florence and Hill

COPING W I T H

Interracial

Dating

Renea D. Nash

THE ROSEN PUBLISHING GROUP, INC./NEW YORK

To Dan: my husband and my soulmate.
Our daughter is a sign that
racial harmony is beautiful.

Published in 1993, 1997 by The Rosen Publishing Group, Inc.
29 East 21st Street, New York, NY 10010

Copyright 1993, 1997 by Renea D. Nash

Revised Edition 1997

Library of Congress Cataloging-in-Publication Data

Nash, Renea D.
    Coping with interracial dating / by Renea D. Nash.
      p. cm.
    Includes bibliographical references (p. 155) and index.
    ISBN 0-8239-2446-7
    1. Interracial dating—Juvenile literature. I. Title.
HQ801.8.N27   1993
306.73—dc20   93-6895
                                          CIP
                                          AC

Manufactured in the United States of America

A B O U T   T H E   A U T H O R ◊

Renea D. Nash was raised in Saginaw, Michigan. The youngest of five children, she often found solace in writing.

She received a bachelor's degree in journalism from Central Michigan University in 1986. After working for newspapers in the Midwest, she moved to Phoenix in search of warmer weather. There she found blistering heat and positions working for corporate newspapers and magazines.

After earning a master's degree in 1993 in mass communication from the Walter Cronkite School of Journalism and Telecommunication at Arizona State University, she went on to work in the public relations department of the City of Phoenix.

On August 24, 1995, Renea married the man of her dreams: Daniel Jude Nichols. On December 8, 1996, she gave birth to their first child, Danni Jade.

Currently, she is a full-time lecturer at Arizona State University, teaching courses in public relations. She is also completing a doctorate degree in sociology.

Contents

Introduction

When I told people I had written a book on interracial dating, I got mixed reactions. Most adults smiled and simply said, "That's an interesting topic." Many wanted to know if it was a "how-to" book. (Can you imagine it: a step-by-step book on how to meet and fall in love with someone of another race?) Others asked if I was "for" interracial dating or "against" it. Almost everyone asked if I had written the book from personal experiences or research. Teenagers gave the most enthusiastic response: "I want to read it!"

The variety of responses revealed a lot to me. Just the mention of the words "interracial dating" made people either visibly uncomfortable or naturally curious. Their reactions told me a lot about them. Mainly, they reminded me that society has not fully accepted interracial dating.

You might be saying, "Hey, this book is supposed to tell me that interracial dating is OK." Nope. My job is to present the facts. So if you're hoping this book will say that interracial dating is no big deal, you'll be disappointed. It will not tell you that your parents will approve, your friends will support you, and no one will stare. And it won't tell you that you're right and everyone else is wrong.

I could tell you all those things, but I believe that it's best to tell the truth, even when it hurts. So that's what you'll get: the good, the bad, and the ugly. But always the truth.

Here are a few truths. First, interracial dating is becoming less of a novelty or taboo. Interracial couples can be seen in everything from Calvin Klein and Levi's ads to music videos and movies. Second, people willing to date interracially are now finding each other through personal ads, highly specialized dating services, cross-cultural functions, 900-numbers, special-interest support groups, and magazines. Third, the question of interracial dating and intermarriage would never be discussed in a society cured of the disease of racism.

If you're involved in an interracial relationship, you may be wondering if you've made the right decision or whether you can handle the pressures. You may be feeling confused and disappointed about some of the things going on between you and your partner. You may be receiving some mixed views from families and peers.

You may wonder whether you should take the relationship to the next level. You may not have told your parents yet. Or you may be looking for ways to tell people to mind their own business.

If you're considering getting involved with someone outside your own race, a lot of questions are probably running through your mind. What will people say? How will my parents react? Will our differences matter, and will I be able to handle those differences? While this book focuses on dating between different races, many of the coping skills apply to those who may be dating across cultural and religious lines as well.

Dating someone outside your own race, religion, or culture is not like dating someone of the same race, religion, or culture. Why? That's a good question. This book will help sort out some answers for you.

The first half of the book looks at the big picture on dating and what parents expect of their children. It discusses our increasingly multiethnic society, race relations, and how prejudice is learned. You'll see how that big picture fits in with how we choose our friends as well as our girlfriends and boyfriends.

The second half of the book discusses the possible conflicts—and positive reactions—you'll encounter with your parents, friends, and the people walking down the street. You'll also learn what special qualities you'll need to make this and any relationship successful. I've also included a discussion of what sometimes comes after interracial dating—interracial marriage and biracial children.

Through real-life stories, you'll see how others have learned to cope with their personal choice to date across racial, cultural, and religious lines. You'll hear from teens, adults, and even some parents. You will follow one couple throughout the whole book. Through their story, you will understand the points made along the way as we uncover the attraction, challenges, and realities of dating outside of the lines. You'll be asked to think openly and honestly about their situation and how they handle certain issues.

You don't have to agree with everything written here. Some of it won't apply to you. Take what you want. Leave the rest for someone else. My only hope is that when you've read the last page, you'll say to yourself, "I'm glad I read this book."

The Dating Game

"**I** am a seventeen-year-old white girl, and I've been dating black guys for three years. I don't think there is anything wrong with interracial couples at all. But my mother thinks otherwise. She acts like it's a disease. She doesn't even want to meet my new boyfriend, Scott. She knows she can't stop me from dating him, but I'm not allowed to bring him home. She says that my grandparents would disown me if they knew. I'm very close to them, but I'm afraid to tell them about Scott. I hate racism. I love Scott and want them to know it. I want to tell them, but it's not that easy. It's also hard at school. Some of the black girls give me a hard time because they say I'm stealing one of their guys. But I'm not. I'm just in love."

"I am a black-Hispanic female. I have dated interracially for only a year. Most of my old friends expected me to 'stick to my race.' They made me feel very uncomfortable, as if I were doing something wrong or had some sort of *psychological problem just because I was not attracted to members of my own culture or race."*

"I am an African American woman in a relationship with an Asian man. The attitude where we live has been pretty accepting. I'm more concerned with the attitude of my boyfriend's family. They are very traditional and want their son to marry a Chinese woman. I have met them, but my boyfriend is reluctant to tell them the truth about the nature of our relationship. That really upsets me."

"I am a white male married to a black woman living in Minneapolis. I think that Minneapolis is a pretty good city for interracial couples. You see lots of different mixes of people. I think anywhere you go in this country you are going to get an occasional stare, but here it seems to be more out of curiosity than of disgust, like I have felt else-where. We are both very lucky. Both of our families fully approve and are happy for us."

Parental disapproval. Lost friendships. Secrecy. Stares. If you are involved in a relationship with someone of a different race or cultural background, you have likely experienced one or all of these reactions. And you can probably relate to the people who wrote the comments above, which were posted on an Internet site dedicated to interracial issues.

That's because interracial couples—no matter what the mix—often spark raised eyebrows, disapproval, public debate, and in some areas, violence. Why? That's a good question. To answer it, let's start at the place closest to you: your home.

Take a good look at your parents. What physical and cultural charateristics do they have in common? Are they the same race? Experts say that parents expect their children to follow the dating model they have established. That model is usually one of sameness, not difference.

In some families, differences are valued and cultural diversity is celebrated. The children are welcome to bring home a wide variety of friends. Racial, ethnic, and cultural differences are not viewed as problems.

Even in such families, however, when the friendship becomes a romantic relationship, the parents may be less accepting of their children's choices.

"We tried to expose [our children] to missionaries and foreign students and people of different ethnic backgrounds; yet when our son announced that he was marrying a black woman, it really took us by surprise," Anita Prinzing, who is white, told *Christianity Today* in an article, "Guess Who's Coming to Church?"

Prinzing and her husband are authors of *Mixed Messages*, a book about interracial marriage from a Christian perspective. They discuss their own experiences. Their son and daughter both married African Americans. The Prinzings accepted their "rainbow" family after some soul-searching.

In other families, parents may find different people to be just that—too different. The unfamiliar can be scary. Some people accept only what is familiar—that is, people of their own race or ethnic background, religion, and opinions. If their children bring home anyone who is different, either as a friend or as a date, the parents most likely consider that person unacceptable and forbidden.

And what happens when your parents say "Don't . . ."? If you're like most teens, you want to do what is forbidden. When something is unacceptable or forbidden, it is often more appealing. Some teens will date interracially out of curiosity. Others will do it to rebel.

If you date someone of a different race, ethnicity, or culture just because your parents have told you not to, the results could be emotionally damaging for everyone involved. Starting an interracial relationship—or any other relationship—simply because your parents said not to is not a good foundation for any relationship.

Why does anyone object to interracial couples? In law and theory, we are all created equal. People flock daily to the United States to be treated as equals, to gain freedom and opportunity, and to be judged on their dignity and character, not their race or origin. In law and theory, all people can live as neighbors and attend the same schools while they worship and marry however and whomever they choose.

But that's law and theory.

You probably already know that just because something is written down doesn't mean it is followed and practiced. And just because it's a good idea to consider everyone equal doesn't mean everyone will think that way.

Unfortunately, racism is here, and it's not going away anytime soon. Your parents may forbid you to date interracially because of their own biases.

Parental prejudices aren't the only grounds for parental objections. Some parents who have dated interracially themselves say that they discourage their children from doing the same. Why? It's an adult thing. They've done it and it wasn't easy. They want to spare their children similar pain. Other parents simply try to protect their children from any act that goes against what society considers the norm.

For a large part of society, crossing racial lines is strictly taboo—almost the same as coloring outside the lines in kindergarten.

But what happens when you go outside the lines? Well, in coloring, nothing much. Sure, you've created a somewhat different picture than what's been printed on the paper. To you, the artwork ranks right up there with the Mona Lisa. Others, however, may see it differently. To some, a picture can only be beautiful if the artist obeyed the rules and stayed within the lines.

It is the same with dating. Some people believe their children or friends or neighbors should not date outside racial or ethnic lines. Some view this as violating the rules. They may have a problem with the picture you've created. And some will tell you it's wrong.

Patricia and Vanessa

Summer was over. Patricia had almost finished packing for her freshman year in college. This was a big step for her; after all, she was only seventeen. Because of her outstanding academic record, she had skipped the tenth grade. Ever since she was a small child, people had commented on her level of intelligence and maturity.

Patricia really hated all the attention. In her eyes, she was an average girl who got lucky in the brains department.

Patricia was about to make the biggest move of her young life. She was excited. "We'll be eating breakfast, lunch, and dinner with hundreds of gorgeous guys," Vanessa would remind her. Patricia and Vanessa had been best buddies since junior high.

Vanessa was one of five minority students at their high school and the only child of their suburb's only black family. Vanessa had received a scholarship to attend the same university as Patricia.

Patricia loved her parents dearly, but both were overprotective. They had "made it" and wanted Patricia to follow in their footsteps. Her parents had her entire life planned out for her—the best college, a high-paying job, a successful husband, and adorable children.

The night before, Patricia's parents had sat her down for "the talk." Basically, it was an updated version of their initial talk about boys and sex. This one, however, was slightly different. It was much more serious in tone. When it was over, Patricia saw her parents in a whole new light.

"Patricia," her mother said calmly. "We know you'll do wonderfully in all your classes, but we're concerned about your social life."

"Boys, Mom," Patricia interjected. "You mean you're concerned about my getting involved with the wrong guy."

"Well, you're going to a big school," her mother said, clearing her throat. "There'll be all kinds of kids there, from all over the state. From all over the country, all over the world. It will be a sort of culture shock for you, dear."

Patricia glanced at her father, who wore a blank expression. She tried to figure out where the conversation was going.

"Our community doesn't have the mix of people that you'll meet at the university. We just don't want you to get involved with the wrong person," her mother continued.

"I know, I know," Patricia said, rather impatiently. "Find someone nice, someone who is special. Someone like Dad. I've heard this lecture before. I know about safe sex and date rape, and I have 9-1-1 memorized."

Her father spoke up. "Okay, young lady, don't be sassy. Just listen, would you?" It was one of the few times her dad had ever raised his voice to her. Patricia sighed. She had really lost her patience now, but out of respect she took a deep breath and let her mother continue.

"I know Vanessa's your best friend," her mother said nervously. "But please try to hang around people who have more in common with you, with us. We don't want you mixed up in the crowd she's likely to associate with, especially the boys."

Vanessa? Patricia thought. What's this got to do with Vanessa? What kind of crowd? What boys? Frustration was evident on her face and in her voice.

"Exactly what are you talking about?" she asked. "What the . . . ?" Then a voice came from behind her. It was her brother, Chris.

"They mean stay away from nigger boys, stupid!" he shouted. Then as silently as he had entered, he left.

The look on her parents' faces frightened her. She knew right away that what her brother had said was true.

"Is that what you mean?" she asked. "Is that what this is all about? You don't want me dating black guys?" The anger she felt made her tremble.

"Your brother was wrong to use that term," her mother said softly. "But, well, those people don't think like us. They're different. Those people. . . ."

Patricia couldn't take it anymore. She interrupted.

"Those people? Try African Americans, Mom!" Patricia yelled. "Or how about the word 'blacks'? I don't believe what I'm hearing!"

Her mother cleared her throat. Her dad looked away. Her mother continued, "We know you'll probably never date any . . . any black boys or anyone else who is not right for you, but we just wanted to let you know that . . . we're not prejudiced, honey. We like Vanessa . . . even though she's . . . well, we're just looking out for your safety. You should only date the right boys."

"My safety!" Patricia yelled. "The right boys! Where is this coming from? Who are you? Where are my real parents!"

"It's just not right," her father finally spoke. "No little girl of mine is going to date anyone we feel is unacceptable. I just won't have it, so don't even consider it. End of discussion."

"I'm not your little girl!" Patricia yelled at her father. "Right now I don't even want you as my parents." Patricia stormed out of the room and up the stairs to her bedroom, slamming the door as hard as she could. Then she began to cry.

Moments later, her private phone line rang. It was Vanessa.

"Hello?" Vanessa called out when Patricia picked up without her usually pleasantry. "Patricia, are you there?"

"Yeah. Yeah. Guess what my parents just said to me," Patricia said quietly into the receiver. She then began to tell her best friend what she thought was a horrible family secret.

Patricia was upset by the discovery she made about her parents. But what has she really discovered? Are her parents prejudiced? Are they racist? Or are they merely following their overprotective pattern?

Experts say that parents are motivated by love and a desire to protect their child. They tend to push for a course of action that will cause the child the fewest problems.

But Patricia sees it as a much more serious issue than one of her parents trying to protect her. Patricia has to make a decision about what her parents said. Although she does not feel the way they do, she needs to understand why they feel that way, or at least try to understand. She has never dated outside her race, mainly because her school was predominately white. There was never the opportunity. She didn't know much about other races and cultures, except for what she had seen on television or read in the newspaper. She had never thought about interracial dating, but now her parents had put the idea into her head.

"Wow, that's pretty heavy stuff," Vanessa commented when Patricia had finished telling the details of the conversation with her family. Vanessa didn't know what else to say. She, too, was in shock. Having spent many weekends at Patricia's house, she had never felt unwelcome. "What did you say?" she finally managed to ask.

"What could I say?" Patricia replied. "I was so angry that I stormed out. I can't believe it. I mean, I know racism exists. But in my own house? My parents? My parents are racist. And Chris, that creep, he said the word 'nigger'!" Realizing what an awful term she had just repeated, she quickly tried to bring her thoughts under control. She became apologetic. "I'm really sorry, Vanessa."

"Why are you apologizing to me?" Vanessa asked.

"Well, for my parents and my brother," she replied. "I can't believe they think that way. I'm so sorry."

"Patricia," Vanessa tried to calm her. "You're not responsible for the way your parents think. They have the right to think the way they want. Besides, parents are weird. Unfortunately, you lucked out and got *really* weird parents. I mean, your parents could win the Academy Award for weird," she joked. "But I'm sure they love you—in a weird sort of way."

Vanessa had tried to lighten up the conversation with some humor. It worked. Before they knew it, they were both laughing about Patricia's "weird" parents.

"What do your parents tell *you* about dating?" Patricia asked Vanessa, realizing that they had never talked about interracial dating.

"Well, Andover High isn't exactly a melting pot," Vanessa answered. "I've only dated black guys. But when we moved here from the city, my parents knew the circle of black guys would be smaller. They said that as long as the guy was nice to me and I cared about him, they had no problem with my dating whoever I wanted."

"So why haven't you hooked up with any of the white guys at school?" Patricia asked.

"Patricia!" Vanessa exclaimed. "It's not a game. I'm not just going to purposely go out to find a white guy to date." She paused. "Deep down, though, I think my parents would be upset. I think all parents want their kids to follow the norm."

"The norm? Gosh, Vanessa, you sound like a grownup. Where'd you get that from?"

"I read it," Vanessa said, laughing. "Norm means what's considered normal—the standard we all have to follow, I think. And wouldn't you say that it's more normal to see a white girl with a white guy or a black guy with a black girl or a Hispanic girl with a Hispanic guy or a Chinese guy with a Chinese girl or a . . ."

"I get the point," Patricia interrupted. "Buy why do our parents say one thing and mean another?

"Parents are weird," Patricia continued. "When my mom said I should find someone like my dad, I didn't know that she meant just white guys. Maybe I'll start dating a black guy and bring him home for Christmas break. Maybe I'll marry him and have his baby. I'd be like that girl in that old movie we saw in Sociology, *Guess Who's Coming to Dinner?* I wonder what they'd do?"

"Patricia!" Vanessa said, shocked. "You wouldn't!"

Patricia hasn't given any rational thought to her parents' comments. Right now, she's angry, confused, and disappointed. She will have to decide for herself what she believes about interracial dating.

But Vanessa has thought about the issue, even though her parents do not forbid her to date boys of other races. Why is it that some parents have strong attitudes against interracial dating and other parents do not? What are parents really concerned about?

What have your parents said about interracial dating? Have you ever discussed it with them?

The issue of interracial dating has affected both Patricia's and Vanessa's lives and raised a lot of questions in their minds. And neither has ever dated outside of their respective racial lines. At least, not yet.

Changing Ideas

Athough interracial dating is nothing new and is now more acceptable than in the past, how people are meeting is definitely changing. People still meet the old-fashioned ways—at the mall, in the grocery store, at church, or through friends. But today, those specifically interested in dating outside their race have several avenues to explore. People now take out personal ads, go to highly specialized dating services, attend cross-cultural mixers, or call special 900-numbers. There are even special-interest support groups and magazines for people who date interracially.

With the advent of technology, relationships and support for interracial dating can be found on the computer via the Internet. The comments from the beginning of this chapter were posted on the Web site of the International Interracial Association.

Interracial dating has become a fact of life.

According to a Los Angeles Times poll of 500 unmarried people conducted in late June, 1994, nearly 60 percent of all respondents ages eighteen to thirty-four years old say they have dated someone from another racial or ethnic group. From the survey, it appeared that younger people were more open to interracial dating than older people. About 43 percent of people ages thirty-five to fifty-four had dated someone from another racial group, but only 15 percent of those fifty-five and older had dated interracially.

There are many studies showing that young people, like you and your classmates, are more open to the idea of interracial relationships. For example, a poll taken in 1993 at a Massachusetts high school found that 94 percent of those surveyed approve of interracial dating.

People are not staying within the lines. More and more people are open to the idea of dating across racial, cultural, ethnic, and religious lines. It's hard to say exactly how much interracial, interreligious, intercultural dating is going on. But let's take a look at marriage and birth statistics.

According to an article in *Time* magazine in 1993, over a period of two decades, the number of interracial marriages in the United States has increased from 310,000 to more than 1.1 million. The number of Jewish people marrying out of their faith has increased from 10 percent to 52 percent since 1960; about 65 percent of Japanese Americans marry people of other cultures; Native Americans marry outside of their heritage about 70 percent of the time. It's also interesting to note that the number of children born to these groups exceeds the number of children born into homes with parents of the same race. And this statistic does not include interracial couples who have babies but don't get married.

This trend is taking place among all racial and ethnic groups, but with differing patterns for each group. The size of the multiracial population is estimated to be 5 million, according to the Biracial Family Network in Chicago.

This kind of openness is often attributed to environmental and/or parental influences. If you live in an urban area or have parents who are liberal (or free thinkers), chances are you're going to accept many ideas that go against what is often considered the norm—staying within the racial lines.

Much of this willingness to date outside one's race also has to do with the fact that racial populations are changing. In fact, population experts predict that by the year 2000, minorities will become the majority. We are a multiethnic society. Just look at your own circle of friends. What kinds of people do you hang out with?

CHAPTER 2

Circle of Friends

Fridays and Saturdays often signal a party at some-body's house, an all-night rendezvous in the parking lot of a fast-food restaurant, or several cruises down Main Street. All of these things are part of hanging out.

Hanging out is how teens build friendships. Groups of girls go to the mall to check out the latest fashions and the latest crop of guys. A bunch of boys go to the arcade to beat the odds at the newest video game and bet on who will get the phone number of the hottest girl in the food court. A group assignment in history class might force a studious gang to hang out at the library.

All teenagers, from California to New York and from Idaho to Texas, engage in the tradition of hanging out. It's been happening for decades. Your parents did it, whether they admit it or not. When your parents' parents were teenagers, places like the malt shop and the skating rink were favorite spots to hang out. Your parents have prob-ably spent more than a few hours hanging out with friends.

Teenagers of all shapes, sizes, races, and religions hang out. These days they tend to do it together. Take a look at the people you hang out with. Are you all the same race? Chances are, if you attend a racially balanced school, your friendships reflect it. Even if your school is made up predominately of one race but sprinkled with minorities, your friendships and associations also will be sprinkled with people of another race.

When we're trying to develop and build true friendships, we tend to communicate better and have lasting friendships with people who have the same interests— from sports to shopping—even if they're of a different gender or race.

Now take a bigger look. Our population is changing, and as it changes, many schools, especially those in the public system, are becoming increasingly multicultural. New opportunities and rich resources come with living in a multicultural environment. The transition, however, is not always easy. It's part of human nature that we don't particularly like change or people we perceive as different from us. And it doesn't matter if these differences are because of skin color, language, or dress. We need time to adjust and to accept. Unfortunately, some people never adjust or accept.

To help close the gaps that encourage these "us" and "them" attitudes, we must build bridges among diverse student populations. Many schools have created programs for both educators and students. Different races and cultures come together and discuss everything from their own fears to personal experiences with racism. Does your school have programs like these?

When you establish just one friendship outside your race, you're already helping to break barriers and overcome stereotypes. What can you do to encourage your school administrators to create some kind of cultural diversity program?

High schools are usually indicative of tomorrow's society. Racial problems that occur there can be seen as warning signs of developing racial problems around the country.

Let's look at one incident that made national news headlines in 1994. It happened in a small city in Alabama. A high school principal was accused of calling a biracial student a "mistake" and canceled the school's prom because interracial romances had allegedly sparked race fights on campus. Although he reinstated the prom the next day, the damage had already been done. Charges of discrimination at the school surfaced, and the town became racially divided. Groups of white supremacists and others marched through the town. In the end, someone burned down the high school.

This incident wasn't about interracial dating; it was about racism. But interracial dating was used as a scapegoat.

Some believe that if stereotypes and biases can be diminished and interethnic relations improved at a young age, there's a strong possibility that society can avoid problems in the future.

Hanging out with teenagers outside your race is one thing, but dating those teens is a totally separate issue. Or is it? Racism and prejudice often surface when things go beyond friendship. Have you ever asked yourself "Where does racism come from?" or "How does a person turn into a racist?" You may be suprised to know that prejudices are learned.

By the time children are three or four years old, they can recognize their own ethnic background. From that time until about age seven or eight, children can categorize racial groups and label them appropriately. Who teaches them to label groups? Parents do. Whatever the parents think, believe, and feel about various racial and ethnic groups is usually passed on to their children, along with the ABCs and 1-2-3s.

That is how people learn to stereotype others and be prejudiced. Nobody just wakes up one day with the stereotype that all African Americans can dance or all Asians are smart. They have to learn these beliefs, and they often learn them in the home. Believe it or not, some adults actually admit that they were taught to hate another race. Others say they were taught separatism, which is a preference for "one's own kind," and a sense of racial superiority.

The media also plays a part in teaching prejudice. Everything from the news to your favorite sitcom on television contributes to reinforcing stereotypes. Many people are only exposed to other ethnic groups from watching television shows or going to movies. This is a very limited viewpoint. Many people make unfair assumptions based on these viewpoints.

Why don't more people resist these prejudical teachings? The answer: It's easier to "stick with your own kind." There are plenty of people in this world. You can easily find someone who is just like you in almost every way. Why go to the trouble of adjusting to new languages, new foods, new cultures, or new customs? For example, in much of England, people associate only with those of the same socioeconomic class. It simply takes less effort to deal with people who have similar values, preferences, and views.

For the same reasons, many parents prefer that their children date within their own race or culture. They want to make life easier for you. However, some people, parents included, really do believe that people should "stick with their own kind," because they think they are superior. When you interact with only your "own kind," however, you're laying the groundwork for prejudice. Separatism can lead to ethnocentrism, which is an exaggerated preference for one's own group that creates a dislike of other groups.

Parents also want their children to take pride in their heritage, culture, race, or religion, and they encourage contact and relationships only within their group. Can you have pride in your race *and* have a racially mixed circle of friends? Can having friends from other backgrounds stand in the way of that pride?

Parents play an important role in their children's racial attitudes. Even the choice of school, which often has a lot to do with economic class as well as race, may tell the child that he or she is different or better. At the same time, many parents encourage their children to make friends with other kids. They want you to expand your circle of friends so you will grow up to be a well-rounded individual, able to interact with a wide variety of people. They want to ensure that their children learn to respect others. If racism can be taught, can't children be taught to celebrate diversity?

Although your parents and your environment play a major role in your attitudes, you eventually learn to establish your own identity and choose your own values.

The Levels of Prejudice

All of us are prejudiced in some way. Some act on their prejudiced views; some do not. Racism, however, is a much more serious condition: when one believes that a person or group is superior to another because of skin color, physical features, or heritage.

G. W. Allport, a psychologist and educator, has identified different levels of prejudice.

The first level is making prejudiced comments around people who hold the same views. This type of prejudice simply means prejudging something or someone that you don't know. But with education and exposure, you can change your view.

The second level is avoidance: going out of one's way to avoid people from certain groups, even if it is an inconvenience. For example, someone may avoid going to a hamburger shop if Hispanic kids hang out there and instead go ten blocks out of the way to another fast-food restaurant.

The third level is discrimination. Many people are at this level. They exclude members of another group or deny them the opportunity to participate in activities. For example, a white boss may refuse to promote women or minorities, or an all-black club may bar whites from memberships.

The fourth level is physical attack, and the last level, the most serious, is extermination (killing). Fatal events like lynching happen at this level.

If you have friends or parents at level one or two, it doesn't necessarily mean they'll advance to higher levels of prejudice. If they object to your hanging out with people of other races, chances are they'll have problems with your dating those same people. It's helpful to you to recognize the different levels of prejudice. You can then examine what level of prejudice your parents are at and deal with them accordingly. It won't be easy. Confronting people, especially parents and close friends, is difficult— even for adults.

For example, if your father constantly tells racial jokes—a level-one behavior—you could tell him that it makes you uncomfortable when he makes fun of others. You could talk about the friendships you have with teens of other races. You could ask him not to tell the joke, or you could walk away. If you feel at ease educating him about the damage of racial jokes on other people, do it.

If a friend is at level four, however, and has physically attacked someone, you may want to disassociate yourself from that person.

It's always a good idea for your parents to meet your friends and get to know them. Parents shouldn't choose your friends for you, although some would be more comfortable if you picked the kinds of friends they would choose. Parents are funny that way.

Your peers may feel the same way. Everyone has friendships other than friends at school. Trying to bring the two together can be difficult, even if everyone is of the same race. It may be even more difficult if there are racial or ethnic differences between the two groups.

Most often, the best way to handle introducing new friends, girlfriends, or boyfriends to parents and other friends is to talk about your new friend first without reference to race. Talk about why you like them and why your friends and parents will like them. Take a few weeks, if possible, to gradually introduce them to your friend through your positive stories of that person. Once you feel your parents seem to like everything they've *heard* about your friend, you can then tell them of that person's race—if you think it's really important. You may be able to open your parents' minds before they get a chance to close them.

For example, instead of saying, "You should meet my Jewish friend, Gary. He's really cool," say, "You will like my friend Gary. He likes basketball as much as you do. He's really cool." That gives everyone the opportunity to know the person first without prejudice. It will help to break down any possible barriers when the actual meeting occurs.

At your age, you're in the process of developing views of the world and people around you. Chances are you're open to everything and everyone. But it can be hard when your parents or other people around you aren't so open-minded.

Love By Happenstance

Have you ever seen *The Dating Game* or *Love Connection*? You may have seen spinoffs of these popular match-making shows. The concept of *The Dating Game* is simple. Contestants try to find the man or woman of their dreams by asking their would-be dates, usually hidden behind a screen, provocative questions such as, "If I told you I had a headache, how would you get rid of it?" From questions like these, contestants choose their mate. Often the person with the smoothest answer or sexiest voice is selected.

That's one way of finding a date. Video dating services and personal ads are other purposeful, and sometimes expensive, means of finding the person of your dreams, or at least someone with whom to enjoy the latest movie.

You and your friends probably rely on the old-fashioned method—meeting someone at school, at the mall, or through a friend.

Whichever method you choose, the outcome is the same: You have a date. A first date may lead to a second, then a third, then perhaps years of dating, and then possibly marriage. You're probably not thinking about marriage yet, though.

Most likely, the first person you date will not be the person you marry. As romantic as it may sound, it's unrealistic to think that your first love is going to be the love that lasts until "death do us part." Not everyone you date will be your partner for life. Why? Think back to some of the boyfriends or girlfriends you've dated. Can you imagine spending the rest of your life with any of them?

Going steady, having crushes, falling in love, breaking up, falling in love with someone else, then breaking up with that person—that's all part of dating. There are many reasons for dating. For teens who are just beginning, dating may be viewed as something to do just because it's fun. You may be simply testing your attractiveness to the opposite sex. You may or may not be thinking about a serious relationship right now.

Whether your dating relationship is serious or not, one thing remains the same. You probably picked that person because of certain traits he or she has. Did you like your last boyfriend's athleticism but hate his bad temper? Did you like your last girlfriend's great sense of humor but dislike her controlling ways? These things are called traits. With each relationship we have, we learn the kinds of traits we want—and don't want—in a mate, so that we can make the best decision the next time around.

This process that everyone unconsciously goes through helps you gradually develop a mental checklist of all of the traits you like. You may even keep a written list of traits. Imagine keeping a list. Sounds funny, doesn't it? Well, take food, for example. You pretty much know what foods you like and don't like. Your mother and father, by example, have shown you how to go into a supermarket and select items that you want and need. You'll be prepared when you finally move out on your own and have to do your own grocery shopping. With list in hand, you'll head to the market and return with the best selections for you.

Of course, you won't go into the mall and find a guy or girl who matches every trait on your list. But you might decide if you want to end the relationship if the person doesn't have enough of the traits you want.

As you continue to date, you'll meet a variety of people and have to keep adding to and perhaps changing your list. It's also possible that along the way you may discover things about yourself that you never knew. Or you may be willing to experience things that you would never have thought about before.

It could be something as simple as realizing a passion for redheads or dating someone slightly older than you. You may prefer to date only tall guys or short girls.

Some people say that they always seem to be attracted to someone of another race, or that they are drawn to people outside of their race. But to list a race outside of your own as a trait can be dangerous. Your motives may not be pure. For the most part, people don't purposely set out looking for someone of another race to date, although it does happen. Most people meet by happenstance.

For example, there may be more opportunities for interracial dating to happen depending on where you live or attend school. You could be rushing down the hall on your way to class and bump into someone, causing both of you to drop your books. Your eyes meet as both of you reach down to reclaim your belongings. Seeing that you both have the same math book, you realize that you're in the same class but never knew it. You study together one day, then another, and another. Then it happens. You start having feelings for each other. He's white. You're Japanese.

Or you're out with friends at the mall and notice a cute girl. You try to ignore the possibility that you're attracted to someone outside your race—she's black, you're white. But your eyes keep wandering her way. She notices and smiles back. The next thing you know you're saying "hi" and asking for her phone number.

If you're involved in an interracial relationship, do you remember how it got started? Most likely, it was by chance. Maybe the chance encounter caught you a little off-guard. If you're involved in your second or third inter-racial relationship, most likely they happened unexpect-edly as well.

From the moment you find someone of another race attractive and think about dating someone of another race, race becomes an issue. From the moment you decide to pursue an interracial relationship, race becomes an issue.

The fact is, it's hard to have an interracial relationship without the differences in your races or cultures becom-ing an issue at some point. You may ask yourself many questions: How can I be attracted to him? Why am I attracted to her? What will my friends think? What will my parents say?

Although our society has made much progress since the 1960s, you know that racism still exists. You read about the ethnic cleansing occurring in Bosnia in the newspa-pers; you saw the police beating of Rodney King and the racially split reactions to the O. J. Simpson trial on tele-vision. Perhaps racism exists in your own family. That's why you question yourself when you start thinking about interracial dating. And you should. It would be a lie to say that there will be no pressures, outside or otherwise.

It would be a lie to say that people won't stare, gawk, point, and maybe even make crude remarks. It would be a lie to say that race will not be an issue. Everyone, whether seventeen or thirty-five, deals with questions like these.

Maybe you and your partner see nothing wrong with crossing racial or cultural lines. People are people, you say. If you're fortunate, your parents won't have any problems with it. But it might cause problems with your grandparents, your great-grandparents, or your friends. Like it or not, it will probably be an issue for a large part of society. By making it an issue for yourself first, you are sizing up the situation before asking yourself another question: Is this something I can handle?

Remember Patricia and Vanessa from chapter 1? Patricia's parents have told her outright that they don't want her dating anyone but white guys. Patricia feels this is prejudice. She's upset with her family, especially because her best friend, Vanessa, is black. Let's see how the two girls are doing at college.

> Freshman orientation. It's the week before classes begin, when all of the freshman students come to campus and get settled in their dorm rooms. They also meet their roommates and learn from the veterans about balancing schoolwork and campus social life. Patricia and Vanessa live down the hall from each other in an all-female dorm.
>
> "So how do you like your roomies?" Patricia asked Vanessa.
>
> "They're cool," Vanessa replied. "It's kind of crowded right now, but we've gotten along so far."
>
> Vanessa was assigned to a room with four other freshmen, who are all white. The dorm director assured

them that their overcrowded situation was only temporary.

"Did you guys do that roommate-get-acquainted thing?" Patricia asked. Her group had been given a long list of questions that they were supposed to sit down and answer.

"Yeah, we did," Vanessa replied. "They've lived sheltered lives."

"What do you mean?"

"Can you believe that not one of them has ever even talked to a black person before?" Vanessa answered. "And Connie—you know, the really skinny one—has never seen a black person except on television. Can you believe that?"

"Are you serious?"

"I am totally serious."

"What did you say?"

"First, I asked if they were kidding," Vanessa said with a laugh. "Then I didn't know what to say. I mean, how can you live for seventeen years and never interact with any black people? That's weird."

"So are you going to move?"

"No," Vanessa replied. "They have to learn sometime that the world isn't all white. Besides, they think it's 'neat' that I'm living there. They had lots of questions."

"What? Did they want to touch your beautiful, ebony skin?" Patricia asked jokingly.

"Get serious, Patricia," Vanessa laughed. "They wanted to know why I haven't washed my hair during the two days we've been here."

Patricia didn't find the question surprising. She had asked it herself during a sleepover at Vanessa's house early in their friendship.

"So I told them that my hair is dry, not oily like theirs, and it doesn't need washing every day, but I could wash it if I wanted to."

"What else did they ask?"

"Lots of stuff, mostly about my hair," Vanessa answered.

"Did you tell them about your weave? I bet that threw them for a loop," Patricia said, chomping at the bit for more gossip.

"I didn't even go THERE!" Vanessa quickly replied. "I'll have to culture them on that slowly." Patricia laughed hysterically and the girls gave each other a high five. "But they asked some other stuff," Vanessa continued. "Like if I was a good dancer or could sing. You know, the same silly questions you asked."

"The only silly questions are the ones not asked," Patricia replied.

As Vanessa finished organizing her notebook, Patricia looked at the campus map to locate her classes. Tomorrow was the first day of classes. Before long, two of Vanessa's roommates came home.

"Hey, you guys want to go to the rec room and play Ping-Pong?" Connie asked.

Down in the recreation room, it was Patricia and Vanessa against Connie and Becky. As they started playing, two attractive guys entered the room. Patricia missed the ball while checking them out. Vanessa went after it, but it rolled near the feet of one of the guys. He picked it up.

"Here you go," said the blond. He was dressed in blue jeans and a denim jacket.

"Thanks," Vanessa said, not looking at him. She went back to the table with the others.

"Are you guys all freshmen?" the other one asked.

They all answered "Yeah" in unison, sounding like a girls' glee club. It was embarrassing.

"Well, good luck," he said. Then both guys smiled and left through the other side of the rec room. The girls watched them go.

"I bet those guys are from Sherman Hall!" Patricia exclaimed. Sherman was the all-male dorm across from them. "The blond one was gorgeous. To die for!"

"To drool for, too, obviously," Vanessa laughed, trying to resume the game. "You guys should have seen yourselves with your tongues hanging out. Need a bucket?"

"Oh, and you didn't think so?" Connie asked.

"Thaaaankss," Becky said in an exagerrated, childish voice, mocking the way Vanessa had received the Ping-Pong ball from the blond guy. They all laughed, including Vanessa.

"Yeah, Denim had it going on, I'll give him that," Vanessa finally admitted.

"Denim?" Patricia interjected.

"Yeah, didn't you guys notice that he was wearing jeans and a jean jacket?" Vanessa asked.

"All I noticed was his butt," Connie said.

The first week of classes was great. Patricia and Vanessa had managed to find all of their lecture halls except one. Both Patricia and Vanessa had made new friends. Two black girls—both juniors—lived across the hall from Vanessa. They watched out for her as if she were their younger sister. After a month, she had moved in with them and their one white roommate. Patricia made friends with almost everyone at her end of the floor.

One evening after dinner, Patricia asked Vanessa if she wanted to join a group that was going to the movies.

"No," Vanessa said, turning down Patricia's offer. "I want to finish reading my book. And there's a good movie on television."

"You're never going to meet any guys locked away in your room," Patricia had told Vanessa more than once. Patricia seemed determined to meet a guy—any guy. She was always scoping, and Vanessa was sure she would spend much of the movie checking out the guys in the crowd.

Patricia took off and left Vanessa alone, sitting on a beanbag watching television. Once in a while Vanessa looked away from the television to see who was walking past her room. Leaving the door open was something almost everyone did. It made it easier for people to feel comfortable just popping their heads in to say hello. And since it was an all-female hall, everyone felt pretty safe in doing so.

During a commercial break, Vanessa again glanced at the door to see who was passing by. To her surprise, it was a guy. He walked by, then came back and stuck his head in.

"Don't you live over there?" a familiar voice said, pointing to the room across the hall.

"Not anymore," she answered.

"Remember me?" he asked.

At first she didn't, then she noticed his clothes. "Oh yeah, Denim."

"Denim?" he said. "My name's Jack."

Vanessa laughed. "Well, you're always wearing jeans so we all started calling you Denim. No offense. Jack, right?"

"Yeah, Jack," he said with a smile, finding his nickname amusing. "Mind if I come in?"

"Sure, I'm just watching an old western," Vanessa replied, reaching for another beanbag chair for her guest. "Grab a bag."

"Cool. John Wayne is my favorite." Jack sat down and squirmed around until the bag was fitted to his frame. Vanessa noticed that he was rather muscular, and he did have a nice butt, as Connie had pointed out.

"Didn't you live over there with Becky?" Jack asked once he got situated, apparently not realizing he had asked the question already.

"Yeah, how did you know that?"

"I thought you said you remembered me."

Vanessa was puzzled. "Yeah, I do," she said, "from that night in the rec room when you gave me the Ping-Pong ball."

"Yeah, I remember that," Jack answered. "But I met you again in your old room. Becky let me use the phone, and you walked in, grabbed a book, and left again. You said hello to me."

Vanessa hadn't remembered. The truth was, Becky was a little on the wild side. She always had guys coming and going. That was why Vanessa had moved. Vanessa apologized for not remembering him.

"Sorry," Vanessa said, "I guess I spaced that encounter."

"Your name's Vanessa, right?"

"Yeah," she said, surprised. "What else do you know about me?"

"That's it," he said. "But you can tell me more."

Within thirty minutes, Vanessa had told him that she was planning to become a journalist, that she and Patricia were best friends from a small suburb of Detroit, and that they both had received scholarships to the University of Michigan.

"I guess that's about it," she said, ending her story.

"That's enough," Jack replied. "So you're one of those smart girls, too?"

Vanessa laughed. "What about you?"

"Well, I'm a sophomore," he replied. "And I'm on the rugby team. I'm orginally from Florida, but I've lived with my grandparents in northern Michigan for the last two years so I could come here . . . and that's about it."

Vanessa didn't know what else to say. Jack didn't seem to have any more, either. The room was silent except for the voices coming from the television. Then something outside the window caught Vanessa's eye.

"Look, it's snowing!" she exclaimed, darting to the window to see the first snowfall of the season. Jack followed her. "It's only October."

"Wow, it's beautiful," he said.

They stood for a moment watching the snowflakes fall. As each flake hit the glass, it quickly melted. It didn't appear that the snow would last.

"Snowflakes are like people," Jack said. "Each one is very different. But together, they're beautiful."

Vanessa was impressed by Jack's sensitive observation.

"Yeah, I guess you're right."

"You want to go walk around in it?" Jack asked.

"Sure, why not?" Vanessa answered.

Vanessa grabbed her thickest sweatshirt. The two of them headed out the back door of the dorm, leading to the tennis courts. For nearly thirty minutes they sat on a chilly bench talking and watching the snow fall. Once in a while they stood with their mouths wide open to let the snowflakes fall on their tongues.

"You're turning white," Jack said, looking at Vanessa.

"What?" Vanessa said, startled.

"Your hair," he answered and began brushing snow out of her jet-black hair. "Your hair is turning white."

They laughed. Then Vanessa took over the chore of brushing the flakes out of her hair. "Thanks," she said rather nervously. "I'd better get back inside." Within seconds she was up and heading back inside the dorm.

"Hey," Jack yelled, chasing after her. "Wait up." Vanessa stopped and turned around to face him.

"Want to go for pizza tomorrow night?" he asked. Vanessa thought about it for a minute. Actually, she was wondering what a gorgeous white guy like Jack wanted with her.

"No, I don't think so," she finally answered.

"What? Don't you like pizza?"

She nodded her head. "I just don't think it's a good idea."

"What? Pizza?"

"No, this . . . you . . . you and me," Vanessa blurted out.

Jack was quiet. Then he spoke. "Look, Vanessa," he said, slowly. "I've never dated a black girl before, if that's what you mean. My parents . . . well . . . all I know is that I've had fun talking to you, and I think you've had fun too."

Vanessa just looked at him and brushed more flakes from her hair. Jack gently took her hand.

"I like you," he said. "It's just pizza." Vanessa smiled. She liked him, too. His observation about the snowflakes had won her over—not to mention his good looks.

"I guess it will be all right," she answered.

"Great," he said. "Pick you up at seven."

We're never really prepared for the unexpected. Vanessa sure wasn't. The first thing she did was to make race an issue and question Jack's motive: What does this white guy want with me? He had just spent nearly two hours talking with her. Could it be possible that he was attracted to her beauty as well as her intelligence? She had a sense of humor and a sense of adventure. And she liked westerns. He was probably impressed with her maturity as much as she was impressed with his charm, athletic build, and sensitivity.

Why couldn't Vanessa have simply seen Jack as a nice guy who seemed to be attracted to her for her? If he had been black, do you think Vanessa would have hesitated to accept his offer? It's human nature to put up our defenses when something different or unexpected comes along. It's a way of protecting ourselves from possible danger.

Jack seems to really like Vanessa. He told her so. His intentions are sincere: He is attracted to her and wants to take her out on a date. But what if his intentions weren't sincere? What if he wanted to date her only because she was black? After all, he said he'd never gone out with a black girl. Vanessa probably thought about that, too. Not long ago, she had just roomed with four white girls who had never talked to a black person before. They had lots of questions. Jack might only be curious like they were.

We often wonder what it's like to be something we're not or to experience something we've never done. Everyone has a natural curiosity level. We want to know everything. That's healthy. Testing the waters is one way to cure our curiosity, and it isn't always a bad thing. But if Jack is just curious, who will end up hurt when he satisfies his curiosity? His motives, however, appear sincere.

A motive is defined as "an emotion, desire, physiological need, or similar impulse that acts as an incitement to action." Motives are negative or positive. For example, you may need to save money to buy a car, so you get a job. That's positive. Another person may work because they want more money to buy drugs. Their actions are definitely based on a negative motive.

Sometimes we do things for the wrong reasons. When it comes to dating, however, our intentions should be sincere. Part of pursuing an interracial relationship is making sure you're sincere and have genuine feelings for the other person. That's a rule that applies in any relationship. But not everyone is sincere, as you'll learn in the next chapter.

Let's go back to Vanessa.

Vanessa found herself almost skipping down the halls of her dormitory. She was obviously happy about her upcoming date. When Vanessa got back to her room her phone was ringing.

"Hello," she said into the receiver, almost out of breath.

"Hi, baby!" a familiar voice cried out.

"Hi, Mamma," Vanessa replied.

"How are you doing? Are you eating OK? Do you need any money?" Vanessa's mother asked without giving her time to answer.

"Fine. Yes. And no," Vanessa answered. Her mother was good at asking the same questions in the same order. Vanessa waited for the question that always came last.

"Have you met any nice boys yet?" her mother asked, as usual. This time Vanessa had met someone. Vanessa quickly weighed telling her mother about Jack. Her own hesitation worried her, because she knew her parents weren't prejudiced. She shouldn't have thought twice about it. But she did. Her mother took her hesitation as a yes.

"You've met someone, haven't you?" her mother asked with excitement.

"Kind of," Vanessa slowly answered. "But we won't have our first date until tomorrow, Mom."

"Well, is he nice?" her mother asked.

"Yes, mother, he's very nice."

"Wait 'til I tell your father," she said. "He was so worried that you wouldn't be able to find a nice young black boy to date."

"Well, I have to go now, Mom," Vanessa replied, not wanting to get into the issue of Jack's race. "I need to finish up some work."

"OK, honey, call me Sunday night with all the details."

"Yes, Mother."

"And Vanessa," her mother called out.

"Yes."

"Be careful," she said. "I love you. Bye."

"I love you too," Vanessa said. "Bye-bye." Vanessa let out a big sigh of relief as she slammed the phone down and rushed to her closet to find something to wear on her first college date. She was really excited. As she reorganized her closet, there was a knock on the door.

"Hey Patricia, come on in," she said in her cheeriest voice. "How was the flick?"

"You're in a good mood. What's up?" Patricia replied, ignoring her question about the movie.

"I got a date," Vanessa said.

"What!" Patricia screamed. "With who? Who? Is it that Leroy guy from the honors dorm?"

"Ugh, no!" Vanessa replied. Leroy was a black soccer player who had a mad crush on Vanessa from the first day he saw her. She told him that they could only be friends, but he was still trying—hard.

"Then, who? Who?" Patricia grew frustrated.

"Remember those guys from the rec room?" Vanessa tried to refresh Patricia's memory. "You know, the guy I called Denim?"

"No way!"

"Yes way," Vanessa replied. "We're going out for pizza tomorrow night."

"Wow," Patricia exclaimed. Then paused. "He's a white guy, right?"

"Yeah, I know," Vanessa replied. "What do you think?"

"Go for it," Patricia said. "If a black guy asked me out, I'd go out with him."

"Patricia, I'm not going out with him just because he's white," Vanessa explained, heading back to her bedroom. Patricia followed her.

"So you like him?" Patricia questioned, doubt in her voice. "Vanessa, you didn't even think he was that cute when we first saw him."

"I did so!" Vanessa insisted. "But there's more to him than that. We had a long talk and a walk outside when it was snowing. And you know what he said?"

"What?"

"He said that people are like snowflakes . . . each one has its own personality. Together, they're beautiful. Isn't that cool?"

"Oh yeah, let's call Hallmark."

"What is this?" Vanessa asked. "First, you said it was cool. Now you're acting as if I shouldn't go out with him. I don't get it."

Patricia sat on Vanessa's bed. Then she got up again and went to the window.

"You're right," Patricia finally said. "I guess I'm just jealous."

"Jealous?" Vanessa asked.

"Yeah, I mean, when is somebody going to ask me out?"

"Oh, Patricia, it's just pizza," Vanessa said, hugging her. "My mother called," Vanessa continued. "I told her I had a date with Jack, but I didn't tell her he was white."

"Why not?" Patricia asked. "It's my racist parents who have the problem, not yours."

"I don't know, parents are so strange," Vanessa replied, not revealing her mother's comment about finding a "nice black boy." "I'm just going to wait to see what happens." She paused. "And stop calling your parents racist. They're just . . . just confused."

Patricia ignored the comment and changed the subject. "So what are you going to wear?" she asked.

"This," Vanessa replied, holding up her favorite pair of blue jeans and a black turtleneck.

"Blue jeans?" Patricia exclaimed. "You two deserve each other. Anyway, enough about you. Let me tell you about the guy sitting in the row across from us. He was drop-dead gorgeous. I didn't even watch the movie."

"Oh, there's a surprise."

It was by accident that Jack and Vanessa met and then met again. Vanessa attends a predominately white school. Her chances of meeting a white guy were a lot higher than her chances of meeting a black guy. But what about Jack? It was an accident, wasn't it? He didn't set out to meet a black girl to date. Circumstances brought them together, and physical attraction seemed to have pulled them closer. They both learned that interracial dating often, like same-race dating, just happens.

So why didn't Vanessa tell her mother about Jack? And what about Patricia's comments? The first date hasn't even occurred yet, and already race is an issue. What if Vanessa was Catholic and Jack was Jewish? What if Vanessa was from the United States and Jack was from some other country? It doesn't matter if the differences between you and your partner are in the color of your skin, your religion, or the country you're from; the difference has to first be addressed by you. Examining your motives is one of the first steps to coping.

CHAPTER 4

When Opposites Attract

The challenges of interracial relationships and the motives behind them have fascinated everyone from social scientists to talk show hosts for many years. Is it morally wrong? Should races mix? Would you get involved in an interracial relationship? The questions are endless.

A computer search of articles on the subject of interracial or interethnic relationships produces mounds of studies. These studies are often interpreted statistically, not as matters of the heart, but as some kind of phenomenon. About 80 percent of studies concern dating between blacks and whites. Magazine articles sensationalize the problems rather than discussing the love shared between two people.

This fascination with interracial and cross-cultural relationships will likely continue. Most people agree, though, that attitudes on the subject have changed. Many people now accept the idea of two people from different races or from different cultures getting romantically involved. If they don't approve of it, they at least tolerate it. Most would also agree that there is still a long way to go before racial harmony is fully achieved and couples of mixed races can exist without feeling the effects of a prejudiced world.

It's hard to say just how many different race/culture combinations are possible. You've probably seen Hispanic/white, Hispanic/black, Chinese/white, Japanese/black, white/black couples, and lots, lots more.

In fact, nearly one third of Hispanics and Asians marry outside their race. About 80 percent of Italian Americans and Polish Americans, along with 45 to 50 percent of Jewish Americans, marry outside their ethnic groups. Japanese Americans marry non-Japanese Americans about 65 percent of the time.

Again, these relationships probably just happened. But with the many choices available to people interested in dating outside their race (such as personal ads, highly specialized dating services, and 900 numbers), these numbers likely will increase.

In 1993, there were nearly 1.2 million interracial marriages in the United States. Of those, 2 percent were black/other race, 20 percent were black/white, and 77 percent were white/other race.

A black/white couple, however, probably is the first combination people think about when they talk about interracial dating, although the number of marriages between the two races is small. No one knows how many black/white dating relationships there are. This combination also is the one that creates the strongest emotional response in parents, friends, and society. Why do you think that is?

Slavery and Apartheid

The reasons can be traced back to the days of slavery. History books document how white plantation owners bought black people like a farmer buys cattle, often treating them like animals instead of human beings. The United States permitted slavery between 1820 and 1860. You've also probably heard of the term apartheid. It was a policy of segregation and political and economic discrimination against non-European peoples in the Republic of South Africa. Until the early 1990s, South Africa was an entire country of blacks ruled by a handful of whites. Slavery and apartheid are two issues that our society, especially the black community, will never forget. In 1,000 years, people will still say that our society has not fully recovered from the effects of slavery.

In fact, it wasn't until 1967 that the Supreme Court struck down state laws against interracial marriage. This issue will be discussed further in the next chapter. For now, you can see why emotions are often stirred when blacks and whites get together romantically.

Considering the unfair, inhuman treatment blacks have historically suffered at the hands of certain white people, some often find it hard to believe that blacks would be romantically involved with any white person. This attitude could also be said to exist among some Hispanics and Native Americans. Particularly when black and white relationships are involved, it leads people of both races to speculate about motives, considering what has happened in the past. What would these motives be? What is the attraction? Is each person hoping to gain something by crossing racial lines? If it's not love, what are the motives?

This fascination with mixed couples and their motives is frustrating to many people involved in an interracial relationship. If you're feeling frustrated, it's normal, and you're definitely not alone. Mixed couples often feel as if their personal lives are being dissected like frogs or feel as if they are on trial with family, friends, and society.

They would much rather talk about their relationship in human terms, discussing why people from different worlds and races challenge prejudices and taboos to join their lives in friendship and marriage. They would like to talk about feelings, emotions, and pure physical attraction. Isn't that the way other relationships are viewed?

Interracial couples do get to talk about those values—but not until they've addressed the race issue. Why are there so many questions about mixed couples? One reason may be that interracial couples look different, and they stick out in a crowd.

Interracial relationships are on the rise. It's hard to go to a mall or movie theater or look at a music video without seeing a mixed couple. And they come in many ages, shapes, and sizes. Many of these relationships are formed from healthy, romantic motives. It's becoming less of a novelty or taboo.

"People are simply looking for serious relationships and are not satisfied by the quality of people that they are meeting, so they are expanding their horizons," says one personal ad representative in a 1994 article in the Los Angeles Times. "That's why they say 'race unimportant' . . . because they realize that there are a lot of quality people that they may not meet if they are closed."

Unhealthy Motives

But some relationships—more than anyone would like to admit—have been and will be formed for unhealthy reasons and motives, referred to as pathological alliances.

Many of these motives originated from sexual myths. If you date interracially, it's helpful to fully understand what people, especially your parents, are thinking about.

Slavery was abolished decades ago, but blacks and whites are still struggling to exist with each other on equal levels. This struggle is also going on in interracial romantic relationships, especially where sexual relations are involved. Many believe that stereotyping, prejudice, and racism can block out the human factors and cause people to treat each other like objects. In other words, romantic relationships between blacks and whites may still be reflecting racial relations as they were long ago. Two researchers examined pathological black/white alliances in 1984. Some of what they reported is presented here.

For blacks, the white partner may be used as a way to vent rage, to gain revenge, and to punish white society. For whites, the black partner may be used as a way to apologize or make amends for white society's sins against the black race. The white partner may also use the black partner for sexual satisfaction based on myths. This may be hard to believe, but it happens. And people who object to mixed relationships often think they're formed for these reasons.

Take the most common black and white couple, a white woman and a black man. Some white women may seek out black partners because they think black men will be better in bed and better equipped to perform sexually. This kind of stereotypical thinking can be common among people who disapprove of the relationship and are looking for the white woman's motive.

In slavery days, the white man thought he had to protect his woman from the black man, making the black man a forbidden sexual object. Some white women may still consider black men to be a forbidden temptation.

Since whites are still the majority and blacks the minority, it is thought by many that black men may seek out white partners as a way to get revenge. A black man may use a white woman to gain social status that he may feel he couldn't get on his own. He may also use her to show society that he is "good enough" to date white women.

Some black men may also try to exert power and reinforce certain stereotypes. They want to show that they can sexually satisfy white women better than white men can.

An 1996 interview with five members of a high school basketball team brings about a candid discussion on interracial dating. All are black, ranging from the ages of fifteen to sixteen. They attend a racially diverse high school that is 55 percent Hispanic, 27 percent Caucasian, 13 percent African American, 3 percent Asian American, and 1 percent Native American.

All laugh uncomfortably when asked if any of them has ever had an interracial relationship. They point to each other and start rattling off names of girls each has dated.

Wayne is a sophomore. His current girlfriend is Hispanic. He says his parents don't care what color his girlfriend is—as long as she isn't white.

"My mother says a white girl will bring you down," says Wayne. "She says a white girl will take all your money."

Denzel admits that he has dated girls of various races. "I date them all," he says with a wide grin on his face. He has even dated an Asian girl, although he can't remember if she was Japanese, Chinese, or Korean.

Another player, Jay, says that his mother has accepted his interracial dating. His father, on the other hand, would prefer to see Jay follow in his footsteps and date only black women.

"My father always says, 'Why can't you find a nice black girl?'" says Jay, whose current girlfriend is Hispanic. "He always has something to say—always. I tell them that (black girls) are sometimes hard to find." All agree that finding a black girl on their racially mixed campus is difficult. Rather than be dateless, they cross racial lines.

"When black girls see you dating a Hispanic or a white, they get mad."

The boys hit on a hot topic. The combination of a black man and a white woman has black women and black men at odds. Some black women will say the black man is "anti-black," "infecting black blood," or "betraying his race." The issue often arises in movies. It was the focus of Spike Lee's hit movie *Jungle Fever*. In another popular movie, adapted from a best-selling book, *Waiting to Exhale*, a black man divorces his black wife to marry a white woman.

White women involved with black men say they get disapproving looks from some black women. When one white college student walked into a nightclub with her black boyfriend, she immediately had a confrontation with a black woman.

"She said that I was the reason that she couldn't find a good black man to date," the student recalls. "She actually wanted to fight me. I told her that I had nothing to do with her problems."

Some black males become defensive when questioned about their romances with women outside of their race, especially white women. As one black man wrote in a syndicated column appearing in the *Arizona Informant*, a black weekly: "If two people are happy together, they should enjoy each other's companionship, no matter what their race. People, including black women, should direct their energy to fulfilling their own lives and leave others alone."

Some black males, on the other hand, may agree that they are betraying their race. Others avoid the issue by not venturing beyond their own racial boundaries.

Now let's take the less common black/white couple, a white man and a black woman, although this combination is on the rise and being seen more often in the 1990s. For example, actress Whoopi Goldberg has been involved with white men, and African-born fashion model Iman is married to David Bowie, a white rock singer.

Black women are also accused of betraying their race when they date white men. Whoopi Goldberg has taken much criticism for her dating choices. In an interview in *Essence* magazine in January 1997, Whoopi responds to the criticism by saying, "I was married to a black man; he is my daughter's father. Before I met Frank (my current boyfriend), I went out with five different men. And two of them were black. That didn't make the papers because that's not news. I've always gone out with the people who ask me out." She goes on to say, "My relationships haven't always been successful, but when they haven't worked, it's been for lots of different reasons."

The same studies from 1984 on pathological black/white alliances report that a black woman may use the relationship as a way to get revenge to express her lack of respect for whites, or to take advantage of a white man's money. In her eyes, a white man may represent wealth and prestige. She may also use him to achieve social status that she may feel she can't get with a black man. Sexually, she may view herself as better in bed than white women and flaunt it to the white man to gain power over him.

A white man may seek a black partner out of a sense of guilt for the pains caused to black people by his white ancestors. And just like the white woman, a white man may seek a black partner because he sees her as something that was once forbidden.

Finally, all of the potential partners in an interracial relationship may use it to rebel against parental restrictions, taking pleasure in shocking or offending friends and relatives.

These motivations may be upsetting and hard to believe. It can be difficult to see how easily it can be for some people to treat each other like objects instead of human beings—all because of myths, stereotypes, or selfishness.

Most interracial relationships are *not* pathologically based. Most people involved in interracial dating reject these ideas. They do not think in these terms or act out of these kinds of negative motivations.

Part of coping with interracial dating is understanding what others are assuming and preparing yourself to respond to those assumptions. Comments will most likely come from people who object or who may encourage you out of their own curiosity. If you're questioned about your motives, you need to decide who's worthy of a response. A close friend might be; a stranger on the street should be ignored.

Coping with an interracial relationship also means examining your own motives. A twenty-three-year-old Russian woman involved with a black man says, "You have to do some soul-searching and ask yourself, 'Why am I doing this?' You have to make sure there are no underlying factors. And you should do that with any relationship." Where interracial dating is concerned, however, she says that you should examine your motives before you do anything else.

If you're involved in an interracial relationship, have you asked yourself: What's the attraction? Do I really like this person? Am I doing this just to tick my parents off?

Make sure the attraction is real and you're being honest with yourself. Be sure there aren't any unhealthy reasons you're crossing racial lines. This is especially important if you find yourself *always* dating someone outside your race. If you find yourself intentionally crossing racial lines, never seeking someone from your own race, you may want to do some soul-searching. Some say it might be a sign of rejection of your own race.

Is it okay to be attracted to someone because of something you heard about that person? For example, people from other countries are often stereotyped in ways that make them more attractive to Americans. Men from France have the reputation of being romantic. Women from that country are said to be great kissers. Women from Southern states have the reputation of being kind and gentle to men. When you date someone for superficial reasons, you are going for a "type" instead of a person. This can be an unhealthy way to approach any relationship.

Healthy Motives

Pure attraction is a major motive, as in any other relationship, but it should never be the only one. Environment could lead to interracial dating as well. For example, if a black person or any other minority attends a predominately white high school or college, dating options are limited if he or she wants to date within the race. A white person who lives in a racially diverse neighborhood will be exposed to different kinds of people and may become attracted to someone outside the race, merely because of the daily interaction.

Past experiences may lead someone to cross racial lines. Who hasn't simply had bad experiences and vowed never to date blondes anymore, or cheerleaders, or guys named

Jeff or girls named Lisa? In the same respect, we may have had too many bad or unhappy relationships with guys and girls of our own race and open our minds to crossing racial lines if the chance comes along. Why not?

If interracial relationships are formed from negative motives, the situation has a way of correcting itself. Only interracial relationships that have been formed on healthy bases will be able to withstand the outside pressures.

The following suggestions may help you examine your own motives. They appeared in Interrace Magazine, an Atlanta-based magazine that promotes cultural under-standing and examines interracial relationships. We've discussed most of the issues already, but these may serve as dating guidelines:

- Racial slurs: If you think terms like "China Doll" or "Chief" are harmless, you should think twice about crossing the color line. The use of just one racial slur has the power of altering an interracial relationship forever or ending it.
- Imitating/impersonating a different race (or religion): Don't try to be something that you're not. You don't have to "act Mexican" to date a Hispanic woman or man. The same is true for any other race. Be yourself.
- Assuming stereotypes are true for all: It is unwise and dishonest to get into an interracial relationship based primarily on stereotypes (such as those discussed in this chapter). Every person should be appreciated and treated on an individual basis.
- Secret relationships: Hiding or denying to friends and family that you are in an interracial relationship is demeaning and unfair to everyone, including yourself.

- Shock effect: Crossing the line is not a game. Don't do it for attention.
- To have fair-skinned children: Don't laugh—this is a painfully honest reason some black people become interracially involved. Relationships should be motivated by love.
- Better sex: A person's skin color or nationality has nothing to do with that person's performance in bed.
- Status symbol: It can be emotionally damaging to a person's self-esteem to know that the only reason he or she was chosen was because his or her skin was darker or lighter. Only you can make yourself acceptable to others.
- Self-hatred: If you look down on your own people, an interracial relationship cannot fill your emptiness. You have to love yourself first before you can truly love anyone else.
- And finally, being afraid to commit: Only you know how much outside pressure you can take. Discuss issues with your partner so he or she is not left hurt.

Let's go back to the college campus and see what's going on with Vanessa, Patricia, and Jack.

Tomorrow night came quickly. Vanessa spent the whole day grooming herself. She did her nails, shaved her legs, and experimented with her hair. Patricia spent the whole day trying to talk her out of her wardrobe selection.

Patricia had also managed to tell the entire floor about Vanessa's date with Jack. A freshman having a date with an upperclassman was big news. Everyone had seen Jack parade through the halls on his "hunt," although he never really seemed to be attracted to any one person on the floor. They were all attracted to him, and tonight they were all envious of Vanessa.

The fact that Jack had asked out a black girl was the second big news. It came as a real shock to Vanessa's two black roommates, both of whom came from inner-city neighborhoods and predominately black schools. She learned of their opinions without having to ask.

Her roommate Tisha had the loudest objections. "I hear you've got a date with a white dude," said Tisha. "What's up with that?"

"What do you mean, what's up with that?" Vanessa got a little defensive.

"I mean, why are you going out with this white guy?"

"Jack is a nice guy; what's the big deal?" Vanessa replied. "Janet is white. Or did you forget?" Janet was their fourth roommate, a white girl from a small farm community.

"The big deal is that Jack is white and you're black," she answered. "And nobody's kissing Janet. That's a slap in our brothers' faces."

"No brother has asked me out," Vanessa said, momentarily forgetting about Leroy, the black soccer player, but Tisha quickly reminded her.

"My man Leroy has asked you out several times. You think you're too good for black men?" Tisha continued. "This white boy is just using you."

Vanessa could not believe her ears. "First of all, Leroy is a nerd. Second, Jack is not using me!" she retorted. "And what could he be using me for anyway? My money? That's a joke."

"For sex!"

"Sex? Oh yeah, I believe that one."

"You may be a little too young to realize this, but white men have been wanting to sleep with black women since we were slaves."

"We?" Vanessa had to question Tisha on that one. "When was the last time you picked cotton?"

The room fell silent. Vanessa could not believe she was having this conversation. She was visibly upset, and so was Tisha. Their other roommate, Wanda, had heard enough.

"You guys stop this," she said. "Vanessa, you just need to be careful."

"Careful of what, Wanda?" Vanessa was nearly in tears.

"This isn't Kansas anymore," Wanda replied. "College men aren't the same as high school boys. Every man you meet is not always going to like you for your personality. He may just like you because he wants something—like sex."

"I do know that," Vanessa answered, calming down. "But you guys don't even know Jack."

"All I know is he's white," Tisha interrupted. "And that's enough for me. So don't come crying to me when people start calling you an oreo." She then stormed out of the room, leaving Vanessa with a confused look on her face.

"Oreo," Wanda explained, "like the cookie: black on the outside, white on the inside."

Vanessa couldn't help but laugh. That was a new one for her. "So what do you think?"

"I think your business is your business," Wanda said. "If that's what you want to do, then more power to you. But not everyone is going to feel the way I do, and you'd better be ready to deal with that."

"Yeah, I see that already," Vanessa said, and finished getting ready for her date. As she combed her hair, she began questioning her decision again: "Am I trying to be white? Why am I going out with Jack when I never gave Leroy the time of day?"

At Sherman Hall, Jack was preparing for his date. Jack was as nervous as Vanessa, changing shirts twice and debating whether to wear his signature denim or not. His stereo was cranked, and the sounds of Seal blared out into the halls.

Jack finally decided on his outfit. As he dressed, his roommate, Steve, walked in.

"Hey dude, I can hear your tunes at the end of the hall!" Steve screamed over the booming drums.

"I was just trying to drown out all that rap music," Jack said.

"What are you doing, man, you got a date?" Steve asked.

"Yeah, going to the Pizza Pan."

"Big spender," Steve replied, surprised that Jack was going off campus for pizza. "Who's the lucky chick?"

Jack hesitated for a second before answering. He wasn't sure why, but he did. Later he realized that Vanessa's being black was probably a factor in his hesitation, and that bothered him. "You remember those girls we talked to over at Bass Hall that night in the rec room?" he finally answered.

"No, not really," Steve replied. "Wait. Wait. Those freshmen babes?"

"Yeah. Those babes, as you call them."

"It must be the tall blonde," Steve said.

"No, it's the girl who came after the ball."

Steve thought for a moment. "The black girl?"

"Yeah, she's cute, don't you think?" Jack replied, hoping not to get into the issue about Vanessa being black.

"Have you gone crazy?"

"What do you mean?"

"It's bad enough she's a freshman, but she's black too!" Steve said, raising his voice. "And didn't you say your dad was prejudiced?"

"Yeah, he is. I've thought about that too."

"Man, rugby has finally affected your brain. You're playing with fire on this one."

"Yeah, well, if I start burning, at least spit on me, would you?" Jack said with a smug laugh.

"Joke if you want, Jack." Steve seemed more worried than Jack was about going against his family. "Your dad will freak if he finds out, won't he?"

"This is my life, Steve, not my father's," Jack said. He and his father were close, but Jack could never accept his father's viewpoints about blacks, Asians, and Jewish people, although he never challenged him. He didn't hate his father at all. Jack had simply vowed never to adopt his father's racist attitudes. He also never expected to date a black person.

"It's just one date, anyway."

"Yeah, yeah, yeah," Steve said, not convinced that Jack wasn't taking this date a little bit more seriously than others. The truth was Jack took all his dates seriously. "What are you going out with a black chick for anyway?"

"Steve, her name is Vanessa." Jack got defensive. "And what do you mean by that? I didn't expect this from you."

"I don't have a problem with it, but I'm sure the guys on the rugby team will have lots to say about you dating a black chick, especially after last weekend."

Jack had forgotten about that weekend, when most of the team came to his dorm room after practice. They all sat around eating pizza, drinking beer, and watching television. A video came on featuring black models Naomi Campbell and Tyra Banks.

"Those chicks have nice booties," one of them had said.

"I prefer Cindy Crawford," someone one else replied.

"I hear black women know how to treat a man, if you know what I mean," another team member added.

"Yeah, once you go black, you never go back," someone else blurted.

Jack ended the macho-racist discussion by saying, "People are people." That comment got a can of beer poured over his head.

"Who cares? Those guys are idiots," Jack replied. "It's just pizza. And I'm late. Later."

Without another word, Jack grabbed his jacket and walked out the door. On the way to Bass Hall, he began thinking about Steve's questions about why he was going out with Vanessa. She's cute, he told himself. She's smart. She's funny. She's easy to talk to. And she likes westerns. She just happens to be black. So what. So what? Jack, you idiot. Your dad is going to have a heart attack if he finds out. The guys on the team are going to razz you every day. What am I doing? What am I doing? It's your life and you can do what you want.

Jack's thoughts were interrupted when he heard a familar voice.

"Hey guy," the voice said. It was Becky, Vanessa's former roommate. For a moment Jack stood there and stared at her as if he was trying see past her to complete his thought. "Cat got your tongue?" she teased him.

"Oh, yeah, Becky," Jack finally came around. "What's up?"

"What's up with you?" she answered back. "Are you coming to take me out?"

"Ahh, sorry," Jack replied quickly. "But I'm sure a pretty girl like you won't be lonely tonight."

"Gee thanks," Becky said, blushing. "So who is the lucky girl?" Becky had spent the entire day at the student recreation center, so she hadn't heard the news buzzing around her floor about Vanessa and Jack.

"I don't know if she's lucky, but it's Vanessa."

"Vanessa?" Becky was obviously surprised. But she recovered quickly and bitterly. "Oh, so that's why you don't like me—I'm the wrong color."

Jack was shocked at Becky's response since he really didn't know her personally. He only knew of her reputation, thanks to locker-room talk. "No, Becky," Jack said, trying to choose his words carefully, "you aren't the wrong color, just the wrong type. I meant what I said about you being a pretty girl. You really shouldn't try so hard."

Becky was silent. She knew exactly what Jack meant, and Jack knew she knew what he meant. He had simply said it to her a lot more nicely than anyone else had, especially the girls on her floor.

"Have a good evening," Jack said, ending the conversation. He began walking up the steps to Bass Hall.

"Yeah, you too, Jack," Becky managed to get out, her voice cracking. "Tell Vanessa I said hello." Jack threw up his hand, signaling that he had heard her and would do so. "And Jack?"

"Yeah?" he stopped and turned toward her.

"She is lucky."

Jack was now nearly ten minutes late for his date with Vanessa. He hated when other people were late and hated it more when he kept people waiting. As he began his journey down the hall to room 210, Jack noticed his heart starting to race. His hands were sweating. He hadn't been this anxious since high school. He thought to himself: Am I nervous because she's black? Am I doing this just to get back at my dad? Before he could answer himself, he was at Vanessa's door knocking.

"Hi!" Vanessa said cheerfully.

"Sorry I'm late," Jack replied. "Ready?"

"Just about." Vanessa grabbed her jacket from a nearby chair. She smiled at Wanda as she and Jack headed out for their first interracial date.

Look at the different responses Vanessa and Jack got when friends found out they were going out with each other. Vanessa's roommate Tisha was almost hostile when she learned of Vanessa's date with a white boy. She warned Vanessa that the black students at the school would accuse her of trying to be white. Tisha even went as far to say Jack only wanted sex from a black girl.

Why do you think Tisha is so upset when Wanda, Vanessa's other roommate, seems open-minded about interracial dating? Both of them come from similiar backgrounds, and both of them are black. Although the same in many ways, Wanda and Tisha are still very different individuals and have their own minds, thoughts, and opinions. We need to remember that every person has his or her own point of view. We should never assume that everyone is going to react the same way. Wanda did give Vanessa good advice by telling her to be prepared to deal with confrontation.

And poor Patricia. She's jealous because she wants a date, too. She could be a prime candidate for crossing racial lines just because Vanessa has done it. Although this is the wrong reason for doing so, it's the copycat effect. You've probably seen it at your school: two best friends both dating jocks or two best buddies both dating cheerleaders. It's normal to try to be like your friends.

Becky was hurt at first because Jack had chosen a black girl over her even though the black girl was Vanessa, a former roommate and friend. Her reaction probably came more from jealousy than prejudice. She later seemed to accept Jack's choice and even envied Vanessa.

Jack's roommate Steve seemed more concerned with what might be Jack's biggest obstacle if he did get serious with Vanessa: his father. Steve also warned Jack that his teammates, guys he spends hours with each day, would tease him unmercifully.

All of these reactions did one thing: They made Vanessa and Jack question their own motives and the attraction they have toward each other. And that's good, because getting it straight in your own mind will help you deal better with others.

What about others? Should we concern ourselves with what other people think or may think? That's a tough question, especially for teenagers who want and need to feel accepted among peers and friends. Often you may say, "I don't care what they think," but inside you really do. Sometimes we base our decisions on what others think, whether we agree with them or not. Sometimes we ignore what others think and do what we want, whether their points are valid or not.

The healthiest way to deal with "what other people think" is to first make sure you are confident about what you think and how you feel about interracial dating.

Then you're ready to consider the "other people." Are these people important to you? Do you value their opinions? Is some of what they think valid? Does what they think really matter to you? If you can answer "yes" to all of these questions, you should then ask yourself: Am I seeking their acceptance of me or their approval of the relationship? There's a big difference between the two. Think about the differences, which will be discussed in great detail in later chapters.

Vanessa and Jack's simple plan for pizza has erupted into a local debate. What should they do now? They could just ignore how everyone has responded, have their date as if nothing was ever said, and simply never go out again. When anyone asked, they could just say, "Oh, we just went as friends."

That's one way of handling a tough situation: Try to turn back the clock by pretending it never happened. But when we do this, we're not being honest with ourselves. The problem hasn't really gone away, it's just out of immediate view. It's not the way to handle a problem at all; it's a way to let the problem handle us.

So what would you suggest Vanessa and Jack do instead? They should probably talk to each other about what they're feeling and how they reacted to everyone else's reactions. If they decide to let this first date go any further, they can decide together how to deal with the reactions they've had so far and the many obstacles they're bound to encounter.

Let's see what happens.

The drive to Pizza Pan took about ten minutes. Vanessa and Jack filled the time with small talk about how good the pizzas were at Pizza Pan, how the rugby team was having a winning season, and how tough it was going to be getting up for eight o'clock classes when it was only thirty degrees outside.

The place was filled with locals—families with small children and elderly couples—and only two other college students. As they stood waiting to be seated, it seemed like all eyes were on them. Jack cleared his throat. Vanessa checked her watch. Both gestures were nervous reactions.

"Two?" a skinny waitress asked. "Smoking or non-smoking?"

"Nonsmoking, please," Jack replied.

"This way," the woman said as she grabbed two menus on her way to their table.

"I'll be back to take your order," the waitress said, departing quickly.

Jack and Vanessa took off their jackets and buried their heads into their menus. Within seconds, their faces reappeared with a decision: deep-dish pizza with everything except anchovies and two large root beers to wash it down.

As promised, the waitress reappeared to take their order, slamming down two ice waters. She then disappeared, leaving Jack and Vanessa with more time to fill before dinner. Vanessa thought for sure their small talk would begin with some trivial discussion about the restaurant's decor. At least that's what Patricia had predicted. But Jack broke the ice with a compliment.

"You look great tonight," he said. "Black looks good on you . . . I mean, you look good in black." It was essentially the same thing, but Jack thought he needed to rephrase the sentence under the circumstances.

"Thanks, it's my favorite color," Vanessa replied. "Although it's really not a color. You look nice too. Do you always wear Levi's?"

"It's those commercials. I'm hooked," Jack said with a laugh.

"Yeah, I could see you hanging out on street corners singing about your 501 blues," Vanessa commented.

"You have a great sense of humor, you know that?" Jack said. "I like you a lot."

Vanessa smiled. She was very attracted to him. "I like you, too."

For a moment, they looked at each without saying anything. Their faces said enough: They were falling hard for each other. Jack, again, broke the silence with yet another compliment.

"You have the darkest eyes I've ever seen," he commented. "They're beautiful."

Vanessa didn't have a response to that one. Luckily, the waitress appeared with their root beers. She darted to another table.

"Cheers," Vanessa said, raising her glass for a toast. Their glasses clanked together gently.

"Here's to new friends," Jack added. It seemed like a corny thing to be doing in a pizza joint with root beer mugs, but neither Vanessa or Jack felt silly.

"You know Vanessa," Jack began, "I don't think I'm going to be able to be just friends with you. But I don't know if we can be more than just friends."

Vanessa knew what Jack was trying to say. She was about to say the same thing. It was as if her first college romance was over before it had even begun. It was depressing.

"Did anyone say anything to you about going out with me?" Jack continued.

Their small talk was about to turn large.

"You mean because you're white and I'm black?" Vanessa had hit the nail right on the head.

"I think I should tell you something." Jack's voice had a serious tone that Vanessa had not heard in him before. "My father, and pretty much my whole family, is prejudiced."

"Against blacks?" Vanessa questioned.

"Against blacks, Hispanics, Jews—the whole world, if you ask me. I was basically told that blacks were no good."

Vanessa didn't know how to respond or what to think. Here she was out on a date with a white guy who was telling her he was raised to hate blacks. Why was he with her? She sat in silence thinking about a mature response.

"I know what you're thinking," Jack said. "Why am I going out with you, right? But I'm not prejudiced. I don't know why I never thought like him . . . but I don't and I can't tell you why."

It was not obvious to Vanessa that Jack wasn't prejudiced, at least not yet. She started thinking about what Tisha had said about white men wanting black women for sex. Could Tisha be right? She hated to think there was any truth to that notion. She was finally able to speak.

"So why did you ask me out?" she asked. "This isn't a white boy/black girl fantasy of yours?"

Jack quickly replied, "No. I swear. But I have been thinking about why I asked you out. All I can tell you is that I like everything about you. You're really a special person. And it's not because you're black or for any other reason other than that I'm attracted to you. I mean, look at you, you're beautiful."

She blushed but focused on the discussion. "So what do you mean you were raised to hate blacks?"

Jack was careful choosing his words. "My dad said a lot of negative things about blacks. He told me that blacks needed to go back to Africa. He uses terms like . . . well, you know."

"Niggers, right?" Vanessa filled in the blank for him.

"I hate that term."

"Jack, this is crazy. What if we do start dating? What's your father going to say when he finds out?"

"To be honest, he would hit the roof," Jack replied. "But I know I want to spend time with you, even though my father would go nuts."

"Maybe we should just be friends, Jack. I don't want to cause any problems." Vanessa thought she had finally come up with a mature response.

"Vanessa, it's not you. It's my father," Jack replied. He paused for a second out of frustration. "I want to be more than just friends with you."

"But what about your father?"

"I don't know. What do you think? What would your parents say?"

"Well, I used to think that they didn't care who I dated as long as he was nice," Vanessa replied, thinking about her earlier conversation with her mother. "Parents are strange. But I don't think they would react like your father. I might be young, but my parents trust my decisions. Or at least they have in the past."

"Look, before we get any more into this, how do you feel about me?

"Here you go," a voice interrupted. It was the waitress with their pizza. She served it up without really looking at either Jack or Vanessa and darted away. To Vanessa, the waitress seemed to be acting a little rude. She brought it to Jack's attention.

"Did you notice the way people looked at us when we walked in?" she asked. "And our waitress hasn't looked at us at all, for that matter. And we're sitting in the back of the restaurant."

Jack took a quick look around the restaurant. The place was packed with townies. Jack didn't notice anyone paying them any attention.

"Vanessa, you're imagining things," he said. "It's really busy here tonight so the waitress has a lot of tables. And so what if people stare—let them."

"Let them?" Vanessa questioned. "I don't want to be a freak show."

"People are going to stare, so what?" Jack replied. "I'm not concerned about that right now."

"So what are you concerned with?"

"Us. You and me," he replied. "We need to decide if we're going to be just friends or more than friends."

Both of them took small bites of the pizza. Neither one of them was really hungry, but it gave them time to think. Their attraction seemed real. The obstacles ahead of them were still unknown. Tonight was evidence that not everyone was going to be happy about their relationship.

"I don't know, Jack," Vanessa finally spoke. "I just keep thinking about your father, the way people are looking at us, what my roommate said, what . . ."

Jack interrupted her. "What did your roommate say?"

"She said that you were just using me for sex and that all the black students would call me an oreo for dating a white guy."

"You know, I'm tired of people saying that all I'm after is sex from a black woman!" Jack got a little loud. He realized it. "I'm sorry. Why do I have to want something from you? Why can't people accept the fact that we're attracted to each other? If we don't care about what color we are, why should anyone else?"

"You know the answer to that."

"No, I don't, Vanessa. Tell me."

"You're black, I'm white." Vanessa stopped, realizing her mistake when Jack laughed. "I mean, I'm black, you're white. Slavery. Racism. All of that plays a part in this. It's a fact of life."

"I know. It makes me angry that we can't even think about starting a relationship without making race an issue."

"Me too."

"So what do we do?"

"What do you want to do?"

"No, it has to be our decision together."

"I don't know if I can handle this. I want to, I really do. But is it really worth it?"

"If you want to and I want to, then it's worth it. We can't ignore our feelings."

"And what are your feelings?"

"I could fall in love with you." Jack's answer was so quick that it took Vanessa by surprise. Her own answer even seemed to roll off her tongue before she knew it.

"Me too."

"Then let's do it."

"OK, let's do it." They again brought their root beer glasses together for an us-against-the-world toast. As they took a drink, their waitress returned to the table.

"How is everything?" she asked. "We're so busy tonight, I've been running around like a chicken with my head cut off. I haven't been a very good waitress to you guys. I'm sorry."

Vanessa and Jack looked at each other and smiled. "Everything's great," Vanessa answered.

Vanessa and Jack have examined their motives and found their attraction to be healthy and sincere. But they are mature enough to know that their decision will affect others and that others will draw their own conclusions about their relationship. Some couples may decide to part ways at this point because of various reasons. After doing their own soul-searching, they may realize that their motives are unhealthy and the attraction is more of a novelty. To them the pressures, the obstacles, and the confrontations are simply not worth it.

Soul-searching and communicating with each other at the beginning of the relationship are crucial to coping with interracial dating. It's also essential to be honest with yourself and with each other. Like Vanessa and Jack, you may decide that together you'll be able to handle being an interracial couple and face whatever obstacles lie ahead.

Regardless of the combination of partners, it is clear that an interracial couple is likely to find some form of objection or resistance in both of their communities. Some couples embrace interracial love for rebelliousness, escapism, or other negative reasons (as do couples of the same race). As you've learned so far, a lot of it has to do with myths and events that happened long ago. These events have formed the basis of race relations in this country.

Race relations are improving, and many people are working toward racial harmony, but sometimes it may seem that much of society is reliving history and not learning from it. However, where race relations are concerned, it's not just a black-and-white issue.

CHAPTER 5

Celebrating Diversity

P olitical Correctness. Diversity. Cultural Awareness. You've likely heard these terms before. In our society's attempt to recognize that people are different in terms of race, gender, sexual orientation, national origin, and even size, these concepts have cropped up to ensure that respect is given to all. Programs have been established and attitudes have changed—all to avoid some form of discrimination.

Firemen are now firefighters so as not to offend women. Blacks prefer to be called African Americans to acknowledge their roots. The business sector and schools across the country have mandated cultural sensitivity classes. Classic fairy tales have been rewritten to reflect more enlightened times.

Despite all these efforts, our world is still not without hate, discrimination, bias, ignorance, and prejudice. Just look at these incidents:

At the University of Georgia, a student from Singapore had eggs thrown through his dormitory window. A Confederate flag was planted outside the window, along with a note containing anti-Asian slogans.

In California, a Torrey Pines State Reserve ranger discovered several fraternity members from the University of San Diego participating in a cross-burning ritual. The group denied that the incident was racially motivated, apologized, and has discontinued the initiation rite.

In Arizona, fraternity members from the University of Arizona campus in Tucson wouldn't let four black males into their party. A fight broke out and one police officer was killed. All these events happened in the 90s, not the 60s.

Incidents have also occurred on high school campuses. At a Georgetown Prep-Gonzaga High School basketball game, thirty to forty Prep students yelled racial epithets at three black Gonzaga students. "Chimp! Chimp! Chimp!" and "Can't read! Can't read!" were some of the insults the students received.

You may know of similar or worse incidents at your own high school.

Let's take a look at the real world. No one is likely to forget the day in 1992 when an all-white jury found four white police officers innocent of the beating of a black California motorist named Rodney King. The riots, fires, and violence that occurred in Los Angeles after the verdict was announced will forever be vivid memories for all those who lived through it or watched it on television.

In 1995, former football star O. J. Simpson was acquitted of the murder of his ex-wife Nicole Brown Simpson and her friend Ronald Goldman. O. J. is black, and the two victims were white. Race became a major issue in his defense. And the four-hour verdict, deliberated by a predominately black jury, divided the world. In 1997, O. J. Simpson was found liable for the wrongful deaths of Nicole Brown Simpson and Ronald Goldman by a predominately white jury. Many noted the race differences in relation to the verdicts of the two juries.

Every April 20, hundreds of thousands of skinheads march the streets of our country to celebrate Adolf Hitler's birthday and proclaim white power.

On December 20, 1986, three blacks were attacked for being in the mostly Italian American Howard Beach section of Queens, New York. One black man was struck and killed by a car as he fled across a highway.

A black teenager, Yusef Hawkins, was killed in 1986 by a mob of white teens in the Bensonhurst section of New York when he was mistaken for being the companion of a white girl who was known for dating blacks and Hispanics.

In November 1996, 1,400 minority workers filed a lawsuit against their employer, Texaco, claiming that the company reserved the best promotions and biggest raises for white employees. An internal investigation revealed tape-recorded conversations of top executives making derogatory comments about blacks and talking about destroying documents pertaining to the case. Texaco, facing the threat of a boycott, settled the lawsuit for $176 million.

Not only large cities are poisoned with hatred. "Niggers, spics, and chinks, quit complaining and get out" was written on a campus building at a college in Northampton, Massachusetts.

The incidents may vary from campus to campus, city to city, and state to state. They may involve people of different races, cultures, religious beliefs, and sexual orientation. However, they all have these things in common: prejudice, discrimination, and hate.

These outbreaks of racial tension and violence are scary, especially when they occur on high school and college campuses. You and your friends represent the future of this world. Your attitudes and behavior patterns set the examples and stimulate changes of norms and values. It doesn't matter that these incidents are isolated events rather than daily occurrences.

It is a common belief that prejudice is based on ignorance. Being ignorant means simply lacking knowledge about something. If we don't know anything about persons of another race or culture, we automatically think "those people" must be different or weird or have something wrong with them. By educating ourselves, we become more sensitive to cultural and ethnic differences, and we eliminate the unknown, the ignorance, and hopefully, the prejudice. It sounds like a good theory. But when racial tensions and violence break out where this kind of education is supposed to be taking place, the theory falls apart right along with race relations.

You may be asking, how can one or two unfortunate incidents do any damage? One bad apple doesn't spoil the whole barrel, but after eating one bad apple you'll be skeptical of the next apple and proceed with extreme caution before biting into it. Some people may never recover from setbacks. They may believe that one rotten apple means the rest are rotten and throw all of them away. At the extreme, they may never eat apples again.

On the positive side, much of society is trying to do something to ease racial tensions and bring everyone together. The Irvine Unified School District in California in 1987 started interethnic relations programs to help its diverse student population get along. Clubs are being formed. Just as Block Watch programs are forming in crime-ridden areas to take back their streets from gangs, students on high school and college campuses are fighting back against racism. You may have heard of the group Minorities Against Discrimination (M.A.D.).

Some college campuses around the country are adding cultural/ethnic awareness courses, and others are making them mandatory. In this setting, students can learn about each other's history and background. They can answer questions and dispel stereotypes.

Others campuses have established strong anti-hate and anti-harassment policies that prohibit students and teachers from interfering with another student's right to peaceful enjoyment on campus or in the dorm. They prohibit verbal and physical attacks caused by race, color, religion, national origin, or sexual orientation. Many of these regulations on verbal attacks are being challenged in the courts as violating the freedom of speech guaranteed by the U.S. Constitution. However, some school administrators say that such policies are necessary to create an environment in which all races and cultures are respected and diversity is celebrated.

To further help minorities and foreign students assimilate, which means to absorb into new surroundings, school officials have created special on-campus centers, rooms, and even dorms where these students can meet people like themselves. Although the centers are open to all students, some nonminority students feel that they actually create more racial tensions by separating people into categories.

It's no secret that the world is changing. In the United States two groups are growing the fastest: Asian Americans and Hispanics. Blacks are no longer the majority among minorities. Population statistics indicate that by the year 2000, blacks, Hispanics, Native Americans, and Asians will account for more than 50 percent of the population of the United States, making them closer to the majority than the minority. Some areas, such as Los Angeles, New York, Chicago, Dallas, and San Antonio, have already reached that point. As society becomes more multiethnic, interracial dating and marriages seem almost inevitable.

The one thing that most people probably fear the most is change. But learning how to interact effectively with other groups will bring about successful changes. And as we said in the previous chapter, we need first to understand the history of different ethnic groups.

Rather than try to understand another perspective, many simply choose to "think" they know about each other.

We all have formed stereotypes about other races. Ask some people you know to finish this sentence: "All blacks are . . ." or "All Japanese women are . . ." Use any race or culture. It's also commonly believed by many that all Chinese know karate, all Colombians deal drugs, all blacks have rhythm, all Irish are drunks, all Mexicans drive lowriders, all Native Americans are drunks, and all Asians are workaholics and lousy drivers. All of these assumptions are harmful stereotypes.

Asian American comedian Margaret Cho often began her standup routines with an opening like, "Hi, I'm Margaret Cho, and I drive very well." She would confront anti-Asian racism with a joke that had her being called a "Chink." Her reply? "Hey, Chinks are Chinese. I'm Korean, so I'm a gook. If you're going to be racist, at least get with the terminology."

Although racism is no laughing matter, sometimes people use humor to diffuse the power of certain words and ideas. For example, some people in the gay community openly use the word "queer" to describe themselves. They feel that reclaiming the word will take away its power to be hurtful and homophobic.

Intraracism exists as well—people stereotyping their own race. Among blacks, color has divided the race for decades. Both dark-skinned and light-skinned blacks say they suffer discrimination from members of their own race because of their hue.

Television, newspapers, and movies continue to perpetuate the stereotypes when stories on gang violence depict only black or Hispanic members and stories on the welfare system depict only black women.

Unfortunately, the list could go on and on. You could probably add some stereotypes yourself.

It's all a vicious circle. Instead of getting to really know each other, it seems that whites and nonwhites would rather cling to stereotypes.

So what is causing all this racial tension? Researchers say that much of the tension on college and high school campuses has to do with competition for jobs and "making it" in the real world. You've seen the words "Equal Opportunity Employer" at the bottom of many job listings in the newspaper. You've no doubt heard of affirmative action, an active effort to improve employment and educational opportunities for minorities (women included). Many nonminority people object to these types of programs because they feel the "special treatment" is causing them to lose out on jobs and promotions. In 1995, affirmative action programs came under heavy fire in Congress, and many of them could be eliminated.

But minorities often blame discrimination when they fail to get jobs, scholarships, or promotions or receive poor treatment. As was shown with the Texaco lawsuit, it does happen. But discrimination isn't the cause in all cases. Paranoia exists on both sides. As in interracial relationships, you can't assume that the whole world is out to get you.

Our nation is obsessed with categorizing people. From the day you were born, you were placed in a category:

white, boy; black, girl; Chinese, girl; Native American, boy; and so on. Today, with the increasing births of biracial children, the classification system is becoming more difficult. Parents of biracial children are refusing to classify them by only one race when they are the product of two. Harvard University placed a "multiethnic" category on its 1992–93 admission applications. Other schools will probably follow suit.

Unfortunately, ethnic and racial tensions, prejudice, and discrimination are not erased by the creation of antiharassment policies or the establishment of programs, special rooms, clubs, and more categories. Education is the key.

Your interracial dating says more than, "Hey, look at us, we're in love." It says, "Hey, two people of different races can not only get along but love each other, and no one has to get hurt."

Amy and Scott are a great example of how two cultures can mix. Amy is white; Scott, Japanese American. The two met in a Japanese class at college. "I was always checking him out; I thought he was cute," recalls Amy. The two spent three semesters of classes developing a friendship— both were dating other people at the time. When each one's relationship ended, they gravitated to each other.

Although Amy and Scott can't see many differences between them, they realize that people view them as an interracial couple. The more visually apparent your differences are, the more you will stand out. The more you stand out, the more people take notice. "We were in Tokyo Express and people were looking at me. I said, 'Is there something on my shirt?'" Amy recalls. "Scott said, 'No, I think it's the whole yellow boy–white girl thing.'"

To Amy, her relationship with Scott seemed normal; her family was used to the combination. "People think I (got involved with Scott) on purpose because my brother married a Japanese American girl." Even her boyfriend before Scott was half Japanese.

Amy's parents had no problem with her dating Scott. But they are often asked, "What's with your family and Japanese people?" Amy's parents feel very uncomfortable when they are confronted by questions about race.

Scott's family members were very Westernized; they accepted any race Scott chose to date. He admits that he does have one aunt who would prefer he dated only Japanese women.

To Amy and Scott, they are just two people in love. It wasn't until they took an out-of-town trip to attend a basketball tournament that reality hit.

"I was the only white girl around," says Amy. "I started to feel uncomfortable—there was a cultural gap. I felt everyone was looking at me because I didn't have dark hair or other Japanese features."

After telling about this incident, Amy begins to recall other uncomfortable moments. "One of the first questions everyone asks me is: Do you eat Japanese food?" she says. When she tells them no, she says, the looks she gets are piercing. "They say, 'Oh,' and I get the feeling that they want me to at least make an effort. I feel like they're saying, because you don't eat Japanese food, you're going to have a tough time catching up."

Another incident involved a Japanese friend of Scott's who wanted to know how much Japanese Amy had taken in school. She had taken nearly three years of the language.

"He said, 'It's pretty sad when a (white girl) knows more Japanese than I do,'" Amy recalls. "I felt like he was taking offense because I knew more Japanese than he did. I wanted to tell him that it wasn't my fault that he didn't know his own language."

Scott thinks Amy misinterpreted his friend's comment. "I think he said it more to mean that it was pretty sad that he didn't know it, not that you knew it." Amy still disagrees.

They agree that when Scott's around Amy's friends, he's the minority; and when Amy's around Scott's friends, she's the minority. Both have to learn to feel comfortable.

One way they are able to feel comfortable is by making sure they know about each other's traditions, customs, and beliefs. In short, they have learned how to celebrate diversity.

People who strive for racial harmony and choose to date across racial or cultural lines have chosen to reject stereotypes and prejudice. It's not an easy thing to do in this age. It takes courage and a strong sense of identity. These people have to be strong because they're going against what society dictates is the norm.

CHAPTER ◇ 6

Crossing Lines:
Cultural, Racial,
Religious

R ichard and Mildred Jeter Loving made history in July 1958 by getting married. Although they were residents of Virginia, they were married in Washington, D.C. Richard was white, Mildred was black, and interracial marriages were against the law in Virginia at the time.

Richard and Mildred knew about the Virginia law when they got married. It clearly stated: "If any white person intermarry with a colored person, or any colored person intermarry with a white person, he shall be guilty of a felony and shall be punished by confinement in the penitentiary for not less than one nor more than five years." Interracial marriages were not banned in Washington, D.C., so the couple travelled there to get married.

When the Lovings returned to Virginia, they were convicted by an all-white jury of violating the state's ban on interracial marriage. The judge wrote: "Almighty God created the races white, black, yellow, malay [Indian] and red, and placed them on separate continents. And but for the interference with his arrangement there would be no cause for such marriages. The fact that he separated the races shows that he did not intend for the races to mix." After spending five days in jail, the Lovings were allowed to leave Virginia if they wanted to remain married.

In a landmark decision, the judge's ruling was reversed by the United States Supreme Court in June 1967, and the law was found unconstitutional, along with similar laws in fifteen other states. The Court ruled that the freedom to choose whom one marries is a right protected under the Fourteenth Amendment.

That was more than thirty years ago. Can you imagine the kind of courage, love, and confidence the Lovings must have had to go against not only what was considered the norm, but what was unacceptable by law? Although interracial dating and marriages are not against the law today, the same attitude expressed by the judge in 1958 can still be found in those who object to interracial relationships.

Couples involved in interracial relationships are faced with questions, stares, discrimination, inappropriate comments, and sometimes rejection. Although love, happiness, and acceptance outweigh the negative reactions and experiences, interracial couples say you should be prepared to deal with it all.

Meet Shawn and Heather. Both are in their early twenties. They met in junior college while both were living in a Southwestern state. Shawn is black, and Heather is white. Shawn grew up in a predominately white neighborhood; this was not his first interracial relationship. Although Heather attended a predominately white high school and could only recall one interracial couple at her school, she had also dated outside her race before.

Shawn says Heather approached him at a school dance and pursued the relationship more than three years ago. They were married in August 1992. She says she knew when she met him that he was "the one." They had a formal church wedding where Heather's father happily gave away his daughter's hand in marriage, witnessed by nearly 150 close friends and family members.

The two agree that anyone can get involved in an interracial relationship for the short term. These short-timers often pursue interracial relationships out of unhealthy motives. As was stated earlier, those involved out of curiosity usually do not have what it takes to deal with the outside pressures of interracial dating. But people who've gotten past curiosity, or who want to turn the casual dating into a serious relationship, have to have more substance if the relationship is to survive.

Is there a certain look to someone who dates interracially? You've likely heard or said to someone, "Gee, you don't look like you would date interracially," or "That brother looks like he dates white girls," or "That girl probably dates only white boys."

For the record, no one "looks" like they date interracially. Shawn jokingly says that given a lineup of women, he can tell which one is most likely to date black men. But on a more serious note, Shawn says he can better gauge what kind of reception he'll get by paying close attention to a woman's behavior. "You can tell by the way they act," he says. "For example, when I asked Heather to dance she just grabbed my hand. Girls won't even physically touch you if they don't want to have anything to do with you." He got the impression that Heather was open to the idea of interracial dating.

Although "looks" are unreliable, surroundings are good indicators. People who hang out with others outside their race or attend gatherings dominated by a race other than their own may be interested in dating interracially. People who date interracially are not visibly different from anyone else. They do, however, think a bit more openly than those who are against interracial dating or wouldn't have the "guts" to do it.

Let's talk about "guts" for a moment. "Guts" is defined in *Webster's Ninth New Collegiate Dictionary* as "fortitude and stamina in coping with what alarms, repels or discourages." Simply put: courage.

Do you think it takes "guts" to date interracially? Maybe the next question will help you answer: Do you think that your dating someone outside of your race, whatever that race may be, has any chances of alarming or repelling anyone you know or may come across? If you say yes, then it will probably take courage or guts for you to continue the relationship and be successful in maintaining the relationship.

Some couples feel that certain interracial mixes may take more guts than others because the mix may not be as common as others.

"You don't see that many white guys with black girls," says Shawn. "So when I do see a couple like that, I say, 'Wow, that takes guts.' "

Historically, when talking about interracial couples, black man-white woman combinations are discussed, even though many other types exist. Within a given race, the definition is probably different. What is considered an interracial couple in your culture or race?

Shawn and Heather say the people who should be considered truly gutsy are those who bravely dated interracially in the 1960s and 1970s, when much of the country was still trying to come to grips with the civil rights movement and the assassination of its leader, Martin Luther King, Jr.

Shawn and Heather respect Richard and Mildred Jeter Loving's fight to stay together. It paved the way for couples like them. "When I meet kids now who have interracial parents, I think, 'Wow, that took a lot of guts (for their parents) to date back then,'" says Heather. "I don't see what we're doing as having guts."

Although the law was on her side, she had another reason for feeling this way. Heather's parents didn't object to her dating Shawn. They had not forbidden it. She adds, "That would have been the hardest thing, if my family (had) disapproved."

"She wouldn't have done it," Shawn interjects.

"He's right," Heather agrees. "I don't think I would be here today." Then she thought about it for a moment. "But true love rules out, so I guess eventually I would have (gone against my parents). I guess that would have taken guts." Heather now realizes how "having guts" plays a role in interracial dating.

It takes guts or courage to do a lot of things in life—sky diving, hang gliding, and bungee-cord jumping. However, not everything that takes courage is life-threatening. Things of this nature include trying out for the football team even though you're 5'5" and weigh 120 pounds, asking someone out on a date when you're really unsure if the person likes you, or standing up to your parents when you really believe you're right and they're wrong.

Whenever you do anything outside of what is considered normal or stand up for yourself against others, it takes some degree of pure courage or guts.

Does having guts mean you're going to be successful at landing safely from a freefall out of the sky, making the football team, or winning an argument? Does it mean you're going to be successful at interracial dating? Many other important qualities can help us when we take risks and display courage.

What about self-esteem? Self-confidence? Independence? A strong will? Attitude? Maturity? Do you think any of these things can add to a person's success in life, including interracial dating? Hint: yes, yes, yes, and yes! And then some.

For teenagers, self-esteem and self-confidence are probably the two hardest things to possess. A lot of adults still haven't discovered the important roles these qualities play in our lives. We all have them—to varying degrees. No one can give us these things. As the words imply, "self" is where they come from. But parents, teachers, or other trusted adults and even books can help us find these things within ourselves, develop them, and use them.

We don't get self-esteem and self-confidence overnight. They don't just magically appear. They develop over time, like your height and your personality.

Outside of reading books about developing self-esteem and self-confidence, we can look to others for example. Such people are called role models.

Contrary to popular opinion among most teenagers, celebrity figures and professional athletes aren't always what adults mean when they say role models. Yes, these people enrich our lives through entertainment or athletic skills, but for most of us, what they have achieved is largely out of our reach. Realizing our own true potential and working within our means is part of having self-esteem and self-confidence.

Self-esteem and self-confidence help us to realize who we are and what we can become and to accept ourselves "as is." We also draw strength from them. A high level of self-esteem and self-confidence is also useful when we are contemplating asking someone out on a date, especially where interracial dating is concerned. Rejection is always possible, as well as negative reactions from other people.

For example, a teenager wrote this letter to "Class Acts," a column through The New York Times Syndicate:

"I'm seventeen and black. My main problem is that I like this white girl at my school, but I think it's impossible for me and her to get together. We are from totally different backgrounds. She seems approachable, but I find it impossible to talk with her. Everyone knows me as a guy who usually isn't shy, but I am. I know if I acted on my feelings for this girl, a lot of blacks at my school would freak out. How do you feel about interracial relationships? What do I do?" He signed it, "In Love."

This teen addresses some pretty typical issues in his letter. What is the tone that surrounds the entire letter? His comments and questions all center around one aspect: fear. He was afraid to talk to her, demonstrating a fear of rejection. And he was afraid of what the black students at his school would think, demonstrating a fear of being ridiculed.

Have you been in that situation before? Maybe you're faced with something similar now. What advice would you give? Would you tell him to forget about her? Would you tell him to take a chance? Would you tell him some of the things you read about in earlier chapters: motives and talking it over with your mate?

"In Love" could probably use a little more self-esteem and self-confidence to confront this dilemma. Let's see what advice he did get. The columnist replied:

"I think you need to decide what's more important to you: what others think? How others will react or treat you as a result? Will you ever feel comfortable in this relationship? Does it matter to you? Try to befriend the girl before you drive yourself crazy with indecision. She may have no interest in you and you will have worked yourself up for nothing. Or she may like you. Together you can decide how to face and deal with the many obstacles you will encounter."

Hopefully, "In Love" has a healthy level of self-esteem. He'll need it. Some people who have healthy levels of self-esteem and self-confidence go right after what they want. If they don't get it, they may say, "oh, well" and keep going, or they may try harder. Some people take rejection hard—really hard. They're devastated and view the rejection as a personal attack on their self-worth.

Pursuing an interracial date can be touchy if you don't know how the other person feels about interracial relationships. He or she may be open to the idea or may not. As the columnist advised "In Love": Befriend the person first and take it from there.

That's what Sybil did. In high school, Sybil had a mad crush on Ron. Sybil was black. Ron was white. They were casual friends. Both worked on student council, and they had many classes together. They were also both jocks and talked to each other during breaks at practice. Sybil decided to ask Ron out on a real date. What do you think Ron said?

He didn't say anything; he put it in a letter. He wrote that their friendship was important to him and that he didn't want to "ruin" it by getting involved romantically and taking a chance of it not working. He had just broken up with his girlfriend, a former friend turned girlfriend. He didn't want that to happen with Sybil and him. She could accept that.

But Ron also wrote that he didn't know if he could "handle" what his friends might have thought because she was black and he was white. He wasn't ready to even try to deal with *that*.

When they both graduated from high school and went off to college, they met up again. Guess what? They tried dating; it lasted for a month. They were better off as friends.

So far we've learned that it takes guts, self-esteem, and self-confidence to date interracially. What about the other traits like independence, attitude, and strong will? Where do they come into play?

One question the columnist asked "In Love" was: Will you ever feel comfortable in this relationship?

Many teenage couples (and older couples) say that the first few times they went out on an interracial date, they felt self-conscious because of the racial differences. They felt as if everyone was staring at them, especially older people. It can be uncomfortable, they say.

One of you may notice it more than the other. And you may notice it for different reasons. For example, when Heather and Shawn go out, Shawn always notices the eyes that follow them. Heather doesn't.

"Black people think about it, whites don't," Heather explains.

"Yeah, you're white," Shawn said. "Most of the prejudice comes down on me because I'm black."

If you're white and you get on the bus with your Hispanic girlfriend, and the bus is filled with all Hispanic students, which one of you is likely to feel more uncomfortable?

"Maybe they're staring at you for other reasons," Heather offers as advice. They could be thinking that you and your girlfriend/boyfriend make a nice couple. They could be jealous. There is always the possibility that they do disapprove. "We don't see black and white," Heather continues. "We're just a couple. People look at us because they think we're going to act different or something. Those people are prejudiced, and I'm sorry that they feel that way. Some people care what other people think and are obsessed with stares from others. I'm not."

After a few months of going out, many couples say that they forget about the fact that they and their partner are of different races. Forget? They say it's possible to be *that* comfortable. They know that the most important thing is how they feel about the other person and how they feel when they are together. They became determined not to let strangers upset their lives.

"I don't roll over in the morning and say, 'Oh, there's my black husband sleeping,'" Heather jokes. "I just say, 'There's Shawn, sleeping away.'"

What about when your differences are not visible because you're dating across religious or cultural lines? The same uneasy feelings may occur, especially when it comes time to attend a formal service or family gathering.

One person may feel uneasy if he or she is unfamiliar with any rituals, customs, or traditions. They may feel nervous or look out of place. It may seem as if everyone is watching their every move.

Becoming obsessed with other people staring at you and your boyfriend or girlfriend may mean that you're not comfortable with the differences yourself. You may need to do some more soul-searching about the relationship. The stares could mean many different things. "Try to ignore them," couples say.

If you're feeling "out of place," it may be that you need to learn more about your mate's religion or culture. Try to take part in as many aspects of your mate's religion or culture as you can. If you can't take part, it's still a good idea to learn about them. If there is a language difference, learn the language—or at least try.

You and your mate will have a better relationship if you both make sincere efforts to learn about what makes you different.

It takes a person with a strong will and determination to make the relationship a success, and it takes self-discipline to "turn the other cheek" or disregard any ignorance. Do you have those traits? Will you feel comfortable in an interracial relationship?

"In Love" also addressed the possibility that his black friends might "freak out" if he started dating the white girl. Perhaps what he was really saying was that his black friends may think that he's trying to be something that he's not. And what do you think that is? What is the one thing that "In Love" can never be, no matter how hard he tries? White.

Keeping your own heritage or racial identity is another issue facing those who date across racial or cultural lines. It's almost inevitable that someone will accuse you of "trying to act black," "trying to be white," "selling out to the enemy," "becoming like *them*," or "turning against your race."

Remember Vanessa's roommate using the term "oreo"?

"I keep in touch with my black friends," said Shawn, whose wedding was sprinkled with several mixed couples as well as many black, white, and Hispanic friends. "But sometimes we'll be talking and one of them will make a comment, 'It's not like you're black.' I get really upset at that."

"Sometimes your own race takes you down," he added. Shawn said he also gets the same kind of comments from his white friends who have told him more than once they didn't "remember" he was black. This usually was said after a disparaging remark was made about blacks. That also upsets him.

He says it's important to maintain your own ethnic identity. You can do that by remaining "in touch" and continuing to embrace your community as well as your customs and traditions.

Each race or culture has its own term for "selling out." In Spanish, the terms may have a more vicious bite: "*vendido.*" Or "*un tio taco,*" a variation of the character of Uncle Tom in Harriet Beecher Stowe's classic, *Uncle Tom's Cabin*. Or *una mosca en leche*, a (brown) fly in (white) milk, trying to blend in. A coconut, brown on the outside—where it is seen—but white on the inside— where it counts. Asian Americans may put down one of their own by calling them a "banana"—yellow on the outside, white on the inside.

Whites aren't left out. Terms like "nigger lover" or "wannabe" are often hurled at whites by whites.

Radar, a Hispanic disc jockey, knows all too well how it feels to be called *una mosca en leche*. Although he learned early on about what was expected of him, he lives his own life. Because of it, he often takes grief from his "homies" for his attraction to white women. "Hispanic pride is drilled into you," he says. "When you first bring a girl home, that's when it hits you. They'll say, 'She's a good girl—she's Hispanic. That's the way it's supposed to be.'"

Having pride was not Radar's problem. It was the other expectations that bothered him. His first *real* date was white. His mother didn't approve. She told him, "Hispanic girls are going to understand you better. Try to find a Hispanic girl. Your kids should grow up and know what they are. You should explore your other options," Radar recalls. "The only option was Hispanic."

His relationship with the white girl didn't last too long; the woman's parents didn't approve. "They gave me the cold shoulder," says Radar. "Her parents had an idea of who they saw their daughter with and her future—and I wasn't it."

Although Radar sees no wrong in interracial dating, he purposely avoids African American or Native American women. He said the combination would be a "culture clash." Radar also admits that he thinks children from interracial couples are at a disadvantage. "I have the choice of keeping my bloodline pure," he explains. "But a Hispanic/white boy does not have that option."

Consider the story of Kim, a Japanese American, who says she was faced with an "identity crisis." Growing up in an all-white neighborhood, she had always dated whites and didn't find Asian men attractive. "I always thought I was white," she says. In the eleventh grade, a math teacher actually told her, "You're the first Asian that I've taught who isn't smart."

She describes the Asian culture as being very strict. Academics were placed above anything else. The women were supposed to be quiet, timid, and meek. Daughters lived at home until they married. Kim, a self-proclaimed jock, says she didn't fall into any of those categories. "I hate school," she says, laughing. "There goes that stereotype."

She realized her identity crisis during her first year of college. "It wasn't until I started going to college that I realized that I was Asian." Some students taunted her because she couldn't speak Japanese or didn't "act" Asian.

After some thought, she realized that she had forgotten about *that* part of her heritage. She started dating a Korean student, a relationship that lasted for more than a year. "But his parents hated me because I wasn't Asian enough," she recalls. "(His sisters) would talk to me, but they didn't like me.

"I didn't feel like I fit in," she adds. Finally, she decided just to be herself. Her current boyfriend is black.

Coping with dating across racial lines means you need healthy levels of self-esteem and self-confidence as well as an almost "who-cares-what-you-think" attitude. It also means having the ability to be independent, or simply be yourself—whether with people of your own race or another race. People may refer to you as a "non-comformist," which is not necessarily bad. In this case, it means you don't always follow the crowd or go with what mainstream society considers "normal." Being independent, in this sense, means that you do what you want and what makes you happy.

Your parents play a large role in influencing your decisions. Your peers and friends may play an even larger role. Think about the last time you had to have the latest fashion because that's what everyone else was wearing. Are you just following a trend because your friends are, or do you really like the latest fashion?

Coping could mean ignoring stares, turning the other cheek, and ignoring harassment. Coping could also mean spending lots of time learning about someone's else background, practicing that person's customs, possibly converting to his or her religion (if the relationship gets serious), or learning the language. Are you prepared to do what it takes to cope with dating across the lines— religious, cultural, or racial? Will you be comfortable in the relationship?

It's not all gloom and doom and stares and taunts. You'll read in the following chapter about how friends and family have accepted interracial dating and respected personal differences. You'll read about the new friends you make as well as the ones you may lose.

It's possible to have a successful interracial relationship. It's possible to stay together despite any challenges from the outside. Couples say that it's not worth the aggravation to dwell on the stares and remarks. They say you should think of yourselves as an example of racial harmony; you represent the best of both worlds.

A 1989 issue of *Cosmopolitan* magazine featured couples of racial and ethnic backgrounds: a Vietnamese woman and her Jewish husband; a white man and his black wife; a Native American man and his white wife; and a Chinese woman and her white husband.

Clearly love sees no color.

The article said it took "special individuals" to marry outside their background. It took courage, independence, and fierce determination—plus all of those traits we mentioned earlier—to live by their own agenda and not that of their family, friends, or society.

People who date or marry across racial and cultural lines say that their lives are enriched. They both learn about a new culture, that of their partner. They learn traditions and customs. In some cases, they learn a new language. And because they live so closely with their mates, they learn about the kinds of prejudice the other must deal with—although they know they'll never be able to fully experience another race.

You'll read about a Chinese-American woman named Kay and her husband Jim, who is white. Jim found that he had many more privileges being white in this society than his Chinese American wife. He saw her confronted with prejudice as she struggled through college. "He sees how the world needs to change just by being by my side," Kay says.

For example, people often found it amazing that Kay spoke fluent English. "People would tell me, 'You speak English good,'" she recalls. "And I'd say, 'No, I speak English well.'"

In turn, Kay has learned about the socialization of white men and the pressures and expectations placed on them by society to be "the breadwinner."

"Jim feels a lot of pressure right now because we can't afford a house," she says. "I try to tell him that it's my responsibility too, but it really bugs him."

Love can make people cross racial, religious, and cultural lines. But because they have "crossed over" to something different from what they're used to, problems do occur. They are aware that somewhere down the line the same differences that attracted them may turn into a source of tension. Questions arise about how their children will be raised or what religion, if any, will be taught.

It's not that they don't love each other; it's simply that they both have differences based on their own beliefs and value systems, which grow out of their racial, religious, or cultural backgrounds.

The words printed on the back of Shawn and Heather's wedding program reiterates the point that love may not see color: "In this world of uncertainty and confusion, we have found each other, so different, and yet in so many ways alike. Having the desire to combine our lives with the joys of resolved differences, we have grown together in love and understanding, climaxing in this day. We sincerely thank you, our friends and loved ones, for making our joy complete by your presence, thoughtfulness, and prayers."

Just because you may be blinded by love doesn't mean everyone else is. Do you think you can handle all the pressure from friends and family that come with interracial relationships?

CHAPTER 7

You're Dating Who?

In the 1967 classic film *Guess Who's Coming to Dinner?* the daughter shocked her white, middle-class family with a surprise guest: her new black boyfriend. She had failed to mention his race. She had also failed to tell her boyfriend that she didn't tell her parents about him. "They'll love you," she had told him before the meeting.

Shock was the emotion that overcame her parents. Among her mother's first questions was, "Have you slept with him?"

Psychologists say this is a normal concern for parents when suddenly faced with their daughter's boyfriend who is of another race or culture—and one they possibly consider inferior to their own. The image of *that* person touching or kissing their daughter, or of their son being in love with *that* girl, is often something parents don't want to think about, let alone accept.

You may be saying, "We're just dating." But parents tend to see dates as potential mates, and they think of sex, marriage, and mixed children.

In the movie, the daughter answered her mother, "No, because he wouldn't let me." Unless your parents have a great sense of humor on sensitive issues, humor may be best left out of it, at least for a while.

Telling Your Parents

If you think your parents will object, there are several steps you can take to prepare them. You may want to invite them to school functions. Some parents don't realize how integrated a school is until they attend functions others than football games. This will give your parents the opportunity to see your new girlfriend or boyfriend as part of your crowd—as a human being, not a stereotype. Perhaps they too can see what you see in the person. What about having a group of friends over and including this person in the bunch? It will give you more reasoning power: It may be hard for parents to object to someone they initially liked.

What if you just wanted to sit down and tell them? Consider your reaction to these five possible ways:

A) "Mom, Dad, your worst nightmare has come true. I'm dating someone from the wrong side of the tracks, but I love her anyway."

B) "Mom, Dad, you're going to find this out sooner or later, so I'll just tell you: I'm dating someone you won't like, but I don't care. You can't make me stop seeing him. I won't."

C) "Mom, Dad, my new girlfriend is someone a little different than you're used to."

D) "Mom, Dad, I'm going to tell you something about my new boyfriend. I hope you're not going

to get upset with me. Please don't be angry.
Please."

E) "Mom, Dad, there's something I would like to tell
you about my new girlfriend, outside of the fact
that she is really great and makes me happy."

Before we examine each of those possible ways of
telling your parents, select the one that you would honestly choose or have already chosen. Remember, select
the one that you think is right for you. And be honest.

Now, why did you select that one? Did one seem easier
to say than the other? Did one sound more like something
you would say? Did one contain more of what your
parents would want to hear? Is one the way friends have
told you to tell them? Do you think your parents would
be more understanding and accepting because of the way
you informed them? Examine why you made the choice
you did.

The most popular answer is E: Mom, dad, there's something I would like to tell you about my new boyfriend or
girlfriend, outside of the fact that he or she is really great
and makes me happy.

Let's examine the others before discussing the popular
choice.

Take "A." It is negative to tell your parents that their
worst nightmare has come true and to refer to your
boyfriend or girlfriend as someone from the "wrong" side
of the tracks. You've given them good ammunition to
shoot down the relationship. Following it up by saying,
"*but* I love them," further implies that you think the relationship is wrong.

Take "B." There's a difference between playing offensive and defensive. When you play offensive, you use skill
and talent. When you play defensive, you bully or use

brute tactics to get your way. It is being defensive to tell your parents that "you don't care" what they think or that "they can't make you" do anything. Nobody likes a bully. Saying "you'll find out," implies that you don't want to confide in them.

Take "C." Sometimes the words we use are simply bad choices. Have you ever said something that came out wrong or was misunderstood? Words like "different" can imply that there is something odd or strange about the new boyfriend or girlfriend.

Take "D." To be assertive means you handle yourself with bold confidence; you're not a bully, but you're sure of yourself. Begging your parents not to be angry about something you haven't even told them is an example of nonassertiveness. Your nonassertive attitude may be viewed as weakness in your feelings for your boyfriend or girlfriend. Interracial dating is hard. It's important to be ready to tell your parents how you feel in a strong, confident way.

Now let's examine "E" and the reasons this statement is popular. First, you're telling your parents that you "want" to tell them something. This signals to most parents that you realize that you didn't have to tell them, and you could have kept it a secret, but you wanted to be honest. The reason you wanted to tell them could range from being afraid they would find out from someone else to making the responsible and mature choice. Only you really need to know the reason. Will your parents appreciate your coming forward with something you think or know they may have concerns about?

Second, you're suggesting to your parents that whatever it is you have to tell them should be placed second to the fact that your boyfriend or girlfriend is a great person. Hopefully, your parents have already seen how happy the person makes you. That and well-placed compliments about your boyfriend or girlfriend could change their negative attitudes, if they have them.

And third, unlike the other ways, this kind of statement is neither defensive nor negative; it's assertive. It says that you are mature, responsible, and willing to stand up for your own decisions. It demonstrates confidence.

There are many ways of telling your parents and many ways they can react. Sometimes no reaction is their reaction. But the important thing is to tell them about your relationship. Don't keep it a secret.

Couples say that keeping the relationship hidden is the same as telling the world (and yourself) that something is wrong or that you're ashamed. If you truly want the relationship, then it is to your benefit to explain to your family and friends that what you're doing is okay and that you and your boyfriend or girlfriend are worthy of each other's love. If you keep it a secret, you spend most of your time plotting and lying instead of going out and having fun. The relationship may become like a game with no real honest feelings involved.

Telling your parents is not enough; you also have to give them equal time and listen to their reasoning. The world can be a hostile place. Your parents could be concerned about your exposing yourself to hatred or danger. You need to try and understand their point of view. Your maturity may surprise them enough that they accept your decision. Anything's possible, as long as you tell them.

Here's what one white mother had to say about her son and daughter both marrying black people. Her comments appeared in an article published in *Christianity Today* titled "How Our Children Surprised Us." She said: "We've learned that people intermarry for the same reasons that two white people or two black people marry, and it's basically for love. There are rare exceptions, such as when somebody's trying to prove a point or punish someone or shock someone, but probably no more so than when other couples marry for the wrong reasons. Once I got to know my daughter-in-law and son-in-law as persons, I could really appreciate them. When we get to know an individual, it makes a world of difference."

Only you know your parents—or at least have a pretty good idea of the kind of parents they are, based on your years of living with them. What kind of parents are they?

There are all types of parents, of course; some are authoritarian—what they say goes, no ifs, ands or buts. Some parents are more relaxed than others. Some parents are more strict than others. Some parents spoil their children by giving them everything they want. Some parents can't afford to give their children everything they want. Some parents can afford to give their children anything, but don't.

Some kids' parents are Democrats; others are Republicans or Independents. Some kids have two parents, a mother and a father. Some kids live with only one parent. Some kids' parents are divorced; others have never been married. Some kids live with adoptive or foster parents or legal guardians.

All parents come from different backgrounds, have different childhood experiences and different ideas, and raise their children differently. The fact that your parents grew up in another era makes them think differently than you do. Your grandparents probably think even more differently than both you and your parents. Always remember that as you try to understand an adult's perspective.

What if you've already told your parents about your interracial relationship, and their reaction was less than positive? Just as you want them to see your side, you need to try to understand theirs. Parents pull from their own experience to make parenting decisions. They also base those decisions on articles or books they've read, on advice from other parents or professionals, or simply on the trial-and-error principle. That is important to remember. Just like you, your parents are human.

Conflicts are resolved through negotiation and compromise. You may not like a 10 PM curfew, so your parents may compromise and give you an extra hour on the weekend. What if your parents don't like your dating choice? They may allow you to see that person at school functions but not on a pick-you-up-take-you-out dating situation. Could you accept that kind of compromise?

You may view your parents' objection as insensitive and controlling. Most parents would say that they are trying to do what's best for their children. They may say things like, "You're not old enough to be in a serious relationship," "You're too young to get involved," or "You really don't know what you're getting yourself into." That last comment may be the real issue for most parents, whether they approve of your decision to date outside your race or not. Their concern is a valid one.

Imagine a mother who has married outside of her race encouraging her sixteen-year-old daughter (from a previous same-race marriage) to wait before getting serious with her boyfriend—a teenager from another race. If it was all right for the mother to do it, then why wasn't it all right for the daughter?

The mother has gone through it already—the pressure of dealing with parents, relatives, friends, and society. Perhaps she is trying to protect her daughter from the pain and ridicule she and her husband faced. Perhaps the mother wants her daughter to make sure she is mature and strong enough and has a healthy degree of self-esteem and confidence. She may want her daughter to allow a strong friendship to develop before becoming romantically involved.

In this situation, the daughter maintained a platonic friendship with the young man. A few years later, she announced to her parents that they were ready to embark on a serious romantic relationship. They were confident that they understood the complications and the rewards that come with an interracial relationship. The mother was pleased.

Part of coping is realizing that every situation, and every parent, is different. You have to handle telling your parents the way you think is best for you, taking all of the above information into consideration and selecting the parts that will help you best.

Julie

Julie was sixteen when she went to a summer camp for gifted students from across the state. She grew up in a predominately white, affluent suburban town. The thought of dating someone black never occurred to her, although she had been friendly with a few blacks at camp.

Then she met Oscar, a black male from a blue-collar family. He was actually from her hometown, but lived in a different neighborhood. They started dating after the first week, and by the end of the summer their relationship was pretty serious.

When Julie went home at the end of the summer, she told her family all about the great guy she had met at camp and announced that they were boyfriend and girlfriend. She didn't tell them Oscar was black.

She thought it would be better if her family got used to the initial shock of her having her first real boyfriend.

The relationship continued for nearly one year without her parents ever meeting Oscar. She always met him somewhere or was outside waiting for him when he pulled up to take her out.

Near the end of her junior year of high school, her sister had a baby, her parents' first grandchild. Her parents planned a big party for the baby's christening. They asked Julie if she wanted to bring Oscar. She thought it was about time they had met him.

Oscar agreed to go but was very upset to learn that Julie hadn't told her parents that he was black. He accused her of being ashamed of him. She explained that she wanted her parents to like him without passing judgment on him first because of his race.

They were the last to arrive at the party, and their entrance was more than grand when her parents' mouths dropped open in shock upon seeing Oscar. They were polite, but Julie knew they weren't happy. As soon as her mother got a chance, she pulled Julie aside and into the kitchen.

"Now I see why you've been avoiding introducing Oscar to us," she screamed. "Have you lost your mind? Don't you know you could never be happy with his kind?"

Julie was so upset with her mother's attitude, she stormed out of the kitchen. Her father was so angry that he didn't say one word, although his facial expression spoke volumes.

Her parents weren't the only ones who reacted negatively. Her eighty-year-old great-aunt had a few words. "What do you think would happen if you and that boyfriend of yours ever had children? Don't expect this family to throw a party for your little black baby!"

"Shut up and mind your own business," Julie screamed at her.

Oscar was upset by the tension in the house. He told Julie that if her family couldn't accept him, then he wouldn't force his company on them. They left the party.

Let's examine what has happened so far. What were all the positive things Julie did? She "talked up" Oscar to her family so they would see him as a person. That was discussed in earlier chapters. However, how was that positive turned into a negative? Julie waited a year to tell her parents. Waiting a month or two would have been more acceptable. Many couples have made the same mistake.

Julie also failed to tell Oscar that she hadn't told her parents he was black. She hadn't even discussed with Oscar how they should handle the fact that their relationship could be an issue. Was she fair to her parents? Was she fair to Oscar or the relationship? Decisions like that have to be discussed and made by both parties.

What about her timing? It wasn't the best decision to drop that kind of bomb on her parents in the middle of a family gathering. It backfired right in Julie's face.

Finally, let's look at Julie's reaction. She told her great-aunt to "shut up." Without a doubt, her great-aunt made a rude and offensive remark, but Julie's response was neither mature nor respectful.

That summer, Julie's parents refused to let her go back to camp, knowing she would be spending three months alone with Oscar. Julie begged, but they wouldn't send her. She ended up working at an ice-cream parlor instead. She was miserable.

She called Oscar at camp often, and he called her although her parents often neglected to give her his messages. Her mother tried to convince her that seeing Oscar would only lead to trouble.

"You're making a mistake," her mother would say. "I'm trying to save you from yourself."

Her mother also told her she was too young to get serious about one guy. She said society would never accept them as a couple. They were too different. Even their religions were different; Oscar was Baptist, while Julie was Catholic. Julie listened to her mother's attempts to break them up for an entire summer.

When Oscar came back, Julie thought everything would be fine. It was their senior year. They continued to see each other as much as possible. Her parents had forbidden her to see him again, and since Julie had never gone against their wishes, they thought she wasn't seeing him anymore. But secretly, they still dated.

But Julie began noticing changes in Oscar, and he had even started hanging out with new friends. Unlike his other friends who accepted their relationship, these new friends were unaccepting. They often made disparaging remarks about whites. They didn't want anything to do with "the racist Western culture of oppression."

Julie often got into arguments with Oscar and with his friends over the issue of race. Once they called her a "redneck," and Oscar didn't defend her. A black female friend of Oscar taunted Julie and told Oscar that he was insulting all of the African American women by dating a white girl.

More and more each day, Julie was losing her family, and Oscar was pulling away from her and closer to his friends. Julie made the decision that hanging onto Oscar wasn't worth it anymore. She no longer had the energy, and he wasn't committed enough to her and the relationship to tell his friends to get lost. They broke up, and they have not spoken to each other again.

Julie doesn't regret dating Oscar, although it nearly destroyed her close relationship with her mother. Looking back, she often wonders if things would have been different if Oscar and she had been the same race or if other people had just left them alone.

But other aspects of their relationship set them up for failure: the secrets, the lack of communication and maturity, and the errors in telling Julie's parents. Also, they both lacked self-esteem and self-confidence. Oscar let his friends dictate his life. Julie ignored Oscar's behavior, standing by and hoping things would change.

Although Oscar and Julie are an example of a black/white couple, this situation could have happened to any mixed couple, no matter what the combination.

Once racial and cultural lines are crossed, the reactions of parents as well as the mistakes made in the telling of the parents can cause many problems. The anxiety attacks, sleepless nights, and internal battles between your heart and your head can negatively affect you and your relationship. Some teenagers are well aware of consequences they will face if they date outside of their race. The same applies to members of various religions who may be forced to leave the family and the church.

Your relationship with your parents will most likely affect the way they will handle your news. For example, Heather was always an independent child. Her parents were used to her doing things that other kids didn't do. She was adventurous and mature for her age. Once her parents got to know Shawn, they accepted him. They saw that she was not just going through a phase.

Heather's brother, however, wasn't as accepting of Shawn. He decided to ignore Shawn, until he learned Shawn liked the same rock group he did, and they became friends. "That freaked him out," Heather recalled. "Now, whenever I go home to visit without Shawn, my brother always asks, 'Where's Shawn, why didn't he come?' And my parents boast about Shawn."

Heather said telling her parents was successful because she was honest with them. Although her parents had never exhibited prejudiced attitudes, she wasn't sure how they were going to handle her news. Not telling them was never an alternative for her.

"Don't give your parents a reason to dislike the person," she said. "If your parents do object, hang on. They may come around."

At first, your parents may see only color or someone whose background or beliefs are too different from your family. But once they meet your boyfriend or girlfriend and interact with him or her, they will begin to see an individual and not just a member of another race.

Here's another example. Remember the young Russian woman who said soul-searching and examining your own motives was part of the coping process? This is how Terri's parents reacted to her telling them she was dating a guy who was half black and half Hispanic.

"My parents were surprised," says Terri, a beautiful, petite young woman with long, dark hair. "Here they had thought they had brought up this wonderful, well-educated, confident child, and she drops this on them. I think they wanted to say, 'Oops, there's something we forgot to tell you: Racism exists and you shouldn't date outside your race.'"

Her parents had sent her to the best schools they could afford, and they took her traveling around the world so she would be cultured and well spoken. They said they did all of this for her so she would have the best things in life. "They said, 'Then you go off and make life difficult for yourself by dating blacks.'"

Her parents said they were simply looking out for her best interests.

"You have to think in terms of acceptance and love," she says of how to talk with her parents. "Don't expect to change their minds. It won't happen."

Instead, she said, she focused on getting her parents to understand that she was her own person, capable of making her own decisions. "Parents have to accept who you are and what you are as well as what you do," she says. "I told them, 'If you love me for me, then you have to accept my decision.'"

She also told her parents that she accepted their position on many life issues even though she didn't agree with all of them. However, she didn't love them any less. That kind of rational discussion got her parents to accept and respect her decision to date across racial lines.

Kay

Kay's parents parents lived by Chinese values and traditions, even after they came to the United States.

Throughout high school she was not allowed to date at all. "You were discouraged from dating, especially outside your race," she says. "Every date is considered a potential mate."

At age ten, she remembers her father telling her that she would be disowned if she ever dated anyone outside of their race. "'Chinese people always marry Chinese,' they told me," Kay recalls. "'Chinese men will never leave you. It would be easier on you and the children.'"

Kay grew up in an multicultural neighborhood in Oakland, California. She had many Asian friends but does not ever remember being asked out by Asian boys. She dated white guys and kept it from her parents by joining clubs at high school that would sponsor events at night—so she could go out on dates.

At age nineteen, she decided to tell her mother and father about a guy she had been seeing for a while. Her younger sister, who was also secretly dating whites, tried to convince her not to tell her father. "'You know what's going to happen,' she said," Kay recalls. "'You're so stupid.'"

She knew that the consequences her father laid out at age ten would still stand nine years later, but she couldn't keep the secret any longer. She respected her parents, had serious feelings about the guy, and wanted to be honest. She came clean, and her father disowned her. "I was considered dead," she sadly recalls. It was like she had never been born.

When the relationship broke up, she was gradually allowed back into the house, although all financial support was discontinued.

She had to pay her own way through college, working two jobs. During her years at college, she met and fell in love with a white student. Again, she knew the consequences.

"You don't select the people you fall in love with," she says.

Again, she was barred from her home. Her father didn't talk to her for a year, although her mother tried desperately to mediate and repair the relationship. Slowly she was allowed back into the house, but she could not talk about her white boyfriend.

Then one day her father needed help repairing the house so he could sell it. He asked Kay if she knew of any guys who could help. She did—her boyfriend Jim. Her father, without hesitation, refused to even consider Jim. "I said, 'Dad, he's real handy and can help you,'" she recalls. "Finally, he had no choice. He gave in."

Jim worked side by side with Kay's father, but the two never said a word. Jim knew the situation was tense. He didn't want to make matters any worse. But when the job was complete, Kay heard something she never thought she'd hear. "My father liked Jim," she says. "He said he was a good person." Jim was finally accepted.

Jim's mother met Kay after hearing about her for nearly one year. He told her that his new girlfriend spoke fluent Chinese and was a great Chinese cook. He assumed his mother would put two and two together and realize Kay was Chinese American.

Kay had no idea that Jim's mother wasn't aware of her ethnic background. His mother met them at the airport. "I could tell by the expression on her face that she didn't know," Kay says, laughing. "(His mother) hit Jim in the arm and said, 'You didn't tell me she was Chinese!'"

"Jim said, 'How many Americans do you know who speak fluent Chinese?'" Kay continues. "We all laughed about it. She didn't have a problem with it at all. She just felt silly because she didn't know."

Today, the two are happily married. Kay has no regrets, although looking back now, she sees what her parents were talking about.

She worries about her children not looking ethnic or being able to pass down the pure culture. She'll have to make sure they remember their Asian heritage. That's probably one of the most genuine concerns people have against interracial dating or cross-cultural dating: loss of a pure culture. But Kay says if she had it to do all over again, she would.

"Kids are idealistic, and sometimes they test their parents," she says. "But you should never write off your family 100 percent. You can't let them run your life. You have to draw a line, but leave the door open, so you can come back or they can come back, and you can repair the relationship," she continues. "When you're young, it's hard to accept the advice of older people, but you should respect it, especially from parents of color. They've lived through a lot."

Not every story has such a happy ending. But talking up your mate, being honest with your family, and giving them time to accept your decision will help you cope.

A lot may also depend not just on the color of your mate's skin but on the content of his or her character. You may purposely choose a boyfriend or girlfriend who will displease your parents. But the shock value is not worth the grief you may cause. You may continue to date the person because of this sense of power you feel you have over your parents. But this is not a positive form of inter-racial dating.

Dealing with Your Friends

Interracial couples say their relationships not only tested their inner strength but helped them distinguish between friend and foe.

Friend is defined by Webster as "one attached to another by affection or esteem, one that is not hostile." Foe is defined as "one who has personal enmity (hatred) for another, one who opposes on principle."

"You really find out who your friends are," says Heather. "If they have a problem with it, get rid of them. They aren't your friends anyway."

Getting "rid" of friends may be hard and painful to do. Choosing between a friend of five years and a boyfriend or girlfriend of five months is one issue everyone has pondered and cried over. The answers are only within yourself. Prejudiced friends or your happiness?

Coping with interracial dating is not the same as coping with high school math. Here, there are no right and wrongs or theories and formulas to follow. It's all a gray area that each couple has to handle as they best see fit. Reading about others and the suggestions of others is helpful, but eventually the responsibility falls on the individual.

The one thing Heather says she was glad she didn't do was linger on the "What ifs" of her decision to date Shawn. What if my parents don't like him? What if they disown me? What if the kids at school tease me?

What if Heather had decided that taking a chance on her parents' reactions was too much of a gamble? What did she stand to lose? What did she stand to gain? Heather took a chance and gained a life-long friend and husband, her family's acceptance, true friends, and happiness. Nine months after the wedding, she gained a baby boy.

Kim was able to repair her family relationship and have her happiness, too. Terri's parents knew they had created a strong child capable of making her own decisions. And as parents, they could accept them. Many more couples who experienced positive or neutral reactions from family and close friends could fill the pages of this chapter, and this entire book.

But couples like Julie and Oscar could also receive their share of ink. Julie took a chance and nearly destroyed her family relationship. Her time with Oscar was a growing experience mixed with both happiness and pain.

Family relationships are important. Personal happiness is important. Let's go back to Vanessa and Jack. They examined their motives and found them to be healthy and sincere. They had already experienced criticism from outsiders. Jack knew his parents would be their biggest obstacle.

When we left them, they had just had their first date. Let's join them after three months of dating. It's winter break, and Jack and Vanessa are back home with their families.

"Welcome home! My baby!" Vanessa's mother exclaimed, nearly hugging Vanessa to death. "You look so much older."

"Dear, let the child go, she's not breathing," her dad said, saving her.

"Thanks, Dad." Vanessa hugged her father, whose bear hug was just as suffocating.

"Did Jack bring you home?" her mother asked.

"Yeah, he's going to visit his grandparents up north before flying to Florida tomorrow to see his parents."

"Up north?" Her father was puzzled for a moment. "Oh, I forgot. Only white folks are crazy enough to live 'up North' in waist-deep snow and actually like it."

"Dad, you promised, no jokes about Jack."

"Sorry, I couldn't help it," he answered. "Why couldn't you have found yourself a good black boy to date?"

"Daaaaddd."

"Leave Jack alone, he's a nice boy," her mother said in Jack's defense. "That's all that matters."

"You say that now, but wait until your Aunt Bessie from Mississippi hears about white Jack. She'll cut you out of her will—if she has anything to leave you."

"Well, she doesn't, so I'm not worried. Besides, Vanessa is my child."

Vanessa's parents often joked about their less-than-open-minded relatives. They knew that relatives like Aunt Bessie would only attribute Vanessa's interracial dating to their family becoming "high-class city people." But the other members of their extended family would accept it. Even if they did have a problem with it, they wouldn't tell Vanessa's father. He was well respected in the family because of his success. If anyone commented about his position in society, he was quick to say, "You don't have to remind me where I came from because I was there, but it's time to move forward and get ahead."

"Dad, I thought you liked Jack?" Vanessa questioned.

"I do, baby girl. He's a nice young man, and you seem to be happy," he answered. "I would like him better if he weren't so pale." He gave his daughter a wink, and Vanessa winked back. Her happiness was his major concern, but he loved teasing her. However, he never teased her about Jack in front of anyone but the family. He retreated to the kitchen to raid the refrigerator for a before-dinner snack.

"Jack's going to call me when he gets to his grandparents' house, so if the phone rings, I'll get it."

"Yes, Vanessa. I'm sure your father and I aren't capable of answering a phone after all these years."

Vanessa snickered as she gathered her things and took them to her room. It was good to be back home. But she missed Jack already.

And the two-hour drive to his grandparents' house was long enough for Jack to be missing her. At one point, he pulled over and got out the picture of the two of them. Vanessa's roommate had taken it the night they returned from their first date. He placed it on the dashboard. Somehow, he didn't feel so alone. No other girl had ever made him experience the strong emotions he felt when he thought of Vanessa. It was true love.

Finally, he arrived at his grandparents' house. He was so happy to finally get out of the car that he gathered his things in a hurry. His haste didn't stop him from carefully placing the picture in his psychology book. It was the only book he saved from his fall classes. On their one-month anniversary, Vanessa had left a "kiss" on page thirty.

"Let me look at you." His grandmother stopped him at the door, examining him up and down. "You've gotten smaller. Aren't you eating?"

"Elle, the boy's as big as a house, leave him alone." His grandfather's voice was full of authority.

"Hello, sir," Jack said. He waited for his grandfather to extend his hand and then pull him in for a hug. Jack could never tell when his grandfather was in the mood for a hug, so he always let him be the first to gesture. This time he was in the mood.

"Come here, son. You look good," he told Jack, hugging him.

"Thank you, sir."

"My turn, my turn." His grandmother threw her arms around him. "Your mother and father will be so happy to see you. You go get some rest, you have a long day tomorrow."

At noon tomorrow, Jack would leave for Florida. He hadn't seen his parents since August. But his thoughts were on one person right then.

"Grams, may I use the phone?"

"Go ahead, honey, then it's off to bed."

"Elle, the boy's old enough to go to sleep when he's tired. For goodness' sake."

Jack headed to his grandfather's library to make his call while his grandparents debated some more. He was indeed tired, but he wanted to hear Vanessa's voice.

"Hello." "Hello." Two voices answered the phone.

"Hang up, mother," Vanessa requested.

"Yes dear. Hi, Jack. Did you make it to your grandparents' safely?"

"Hello, Mrs. Davis. Yes, I did, thank you."

"Okay, Mother, hang up." Her mother obliged. "Hi, Jack!"

"Hi, do you miss me?"

"You know I do," Vanessa answered. "Do you miss me?"

"Silly girl." It was a tradition for the two of them to start every conversation that way. Wanda said they were still in the "lovesick phase," and it would pass.

"I can't wait for these two weeks to go by," Vanessa said.

"Yeah, me eith—eeerrr." Jack yawned in the middle of the word. "Sorry, babe. I'm really tired."

"Well, get some sleep and dream of me, okay?"

"I'll dream of us."

"You're so sweet. I love you."

"I love you, too," Jack answered.

The next morning came fast. A large brunch was already on the table. Jack quickly showered and got dressed. Conversation around the table had to do with the usual: school, sports, and girls.

"Who's the lucky lady, Jack?"

"Oh, you'll like her, Grams, she's beautiful," Jack answered. He was careful not to reveal Vanessa's race. His grandfather would never accept his choice of girlfriend. Instead, he talked about her mind and her personality. "She's on academic scholarship. She has a great sense of humor. And she likes westerns!"

"Not too many women like westerns, son, you'd better stick with that one." If his grandfather only knew—but Jack was not about to break it to him over brunch.

Jack boarded his plane and had dozed off before takeoff. He woke with the feeling that he had left something behind. Then it came to him: his psychology book, with Vanessa's photo tucked inside.

Seeing his parents at the gate took his mind off forgetting the book. It was a great reunion. His mother cried. His father, almost a carbon-copy of his grandfather, first shook his hand, then pulled him in for a hug.

Jack had other pictures of Vanessa, so he didn't remember the "first date" picture until his grandmother called the night before the end of his two-week break. His dad had answered the telephone. When his dad hung up, Jack knew what their conversation had been about: Vanessa.

"Is this true? Are you dating some nigger?" his father demanded.

"Her name is Vanessa, dad, and she's not a nigger."

"Don't you talk back to me. No son of mine is going to date some nigger!"

The shouting brought Jack's mother running into the room. "What's going on?"

"Your son is dating some nigger girl, that's what!"

Jack's mother turned to him. "Son, is that true?"

"Yes, Mom, she's black."

"Oh, son." Jack's mother didn't have the same prejudiced views as his father, but she never spoke out against them.

"No son of mine is going to date a nigger! That's final!"

There was absolutely no room for discussion on this issue, and Jack knew it. What he didn't expect was what his father said next.

"You have a choice, Jack: Either stop dating her or get the hell out of this family!"

"Paul, no! Jack, talk to him!" His mother was in hysterics. Jack said nothing.

"I mean it, Jack. What's it going to be? Make your choice."

Jack finally spoke, nervously. "I'm really sorry you feel this way, Dad. I've never gone against your wishes, but I can't accept your views. Not on this one. Vanessa is a really nice person who happens to be black." His father grunted when Jack said that. "I don't want to choose between my family and Vanessa."

"It's either stop dating her or get out!" his father interrupted.

Jack kept his composure, but he was trembling and crying inside. "I have to be my own man, Dad. I can't let you control my life. I guess I'll get my things."

"Is that your choice?"

"You've given me no choice, Dad. I can accept you. Why can't you . . ." Jack didn't complete his sentence.

"Don't even say it, Jack. I'll never accept that. You know that!" Jack's father stormed out the door.

Jack's mother, in tears, threw her arms around him. "No, Jack. Just stop dating her. Just stop!"

"I can't, Mom, I love her." He had never said that before to anyone. It was as though the entire episode with his father made him realize how much he wanted to be with Vanessa. Then his thoughts turned to Vanessa.

"I need to make a phone call." He hugged his mother and went to the phone. How was he going to tell Vanessa? What was she going to say? Had he made the right decision without even talking with her?

"Hello." It was Vanessa.

"Hi, do you miss me?" Jack spoke softly into the phone, in a stunned voice that Vanessa picked up on right away.

"What's wrong?" she asked, dispensing with their routine. She didn't wait for an answer. "Don't tell me, your grandmother called your father?"

"How did you know?"

"She called here after she found the picture of us."

"What!"

"She got my number from her telephone bill. She told my father that we were thinking about getting married, and he should make me break up with you."

"I can't believe this is happening. What did your father say?"

"He told her that we were just kids dating, and he was sure we weren't talking marriage. What's happened, Jack?" Vanessa didn't go on to tell Jack that her father asked if his grandmother was senile.

"Well, good ole Grams let the cat out of the bag, and my father totally freaked out."

"What happened?" Vanessa questioned again.

"Basically, my father said to either stop dating you or leave the family. He said no son of his was going to date a . . . you know."

"A nigger, right?"

"God, I hate that word! Don't ever use that word!" Jack shouted.

"Okay, okay, I'm sorry. Then what?"

"Well, I told him I would get my things and go."

There was silence on Vanessa's end of the phone. Tears welled in her eyes. She didn't know how to feel, although guilt was heading to the front of her mind.

"Vanessa?"

Vanessa wiped her tears. "I can't let you do this, Jack. I can't let you lose your family because of me."

"It's not because of you, Vanessa."

"What do you mean? It *is* because of me. It's because I'm black. I can't help that, Jack. But I can't let you do this because of me!" Now Vanessa, like Jack's mother, was in hysterics.

"Vanessa, calm down," Jack pleaded with her. "Look, my father gave me an ultimatum. He pushed me into a corner. Just because he's my father doesn't mean he can run my life."

"Jack, I'm so sorry."

"What are you sorry for? It's not your fault. It's his."

"I just wish you had talked to me before you made this decision. I still feel like it's my fault. How are you going to pay for school? What are you going to do for money? How are you going to eat?" Vanessa was starting to ramble.

"Slow down, Vanessa," Jack replied. "It all happened really quick. I had to react, and I saw no other way out. This is the right decision for me. Are you with me on this one? I can't do it without you."

Vanessa was silent again. Here was a man she had only dated for three months, ready to give up his entire family for her. She was only eighteen. How could she handle this kind of pressure? Could she come between Jack's family? Should she tell him to stay with his family?

"Vanessa, say something."

"I don't want you to lose your family because of me. And what about school? It's not worth it, Jack."

"Vanessa. I know you don't mean that, do you? Do you?"

"No, I'm just scared. Isn't there any other solution?"

"I'm scared too, Vanessa. And it hurts, it hurts real bad," Jack replied. "I do know that my leaving home is not really a solution. But it's the way my father wants

it. I just need to hear that you'll stand with me . . .
you're my only family now."

"Jack, don't say that. You can't give up on your
parents. You have to keep trying. That's the only way I
will feel good about this decision. You have to keep
trying."

"I'll keep trying—with my mother. I don't know what
good it will do. My father is really serious. But I'll keep
trying."

"What have we done?"

"We haven't done anything but fall in love. That's not
a crime." Jack had a good head on his shoulders. He
was strong and determined, just like his father and
grandfather. They had taught him well, maybe too well.
"You know, I told my mother that I loved you. I've never
told anybody that before."

"Oh, Jack." Vanessa started to cry again.

"Don't cry. It's going to be all right. In a way, my
father is bringing us closer together . . . because you're
all I've got now."

"Will things be different?"

"Well, I'll have to work. I may have to quit playing
rugby. But I'll manage," Jack answered. "If I have
to take one class at a time, I'm still going to finish
school."

To Vanessa, it sounded as if Jack had things all worked
out in his mind. Only Jack knew the real panic that was
rushing through his body. He was in pain.

"Now what?"

"I'll pick you up tomorrow at six o'clock. I can't wait
to see a friendly face."

"I can't wait to hug you," Vanessa replied. "Jack, it
looks like we've been pushed into something more
serious than we ever intended. Please don't misunder-

stand that. I love you, and I'm going to be here for you—for us. I just hate that it happened this way."

"So do I," Jack said. "But it'll be okay. It'll be tough going for a while, but it'll be okay. It has to be. Get some sleep."

"Dream of us," Vanessa said.

"That's all I can do."

Vanessa could hear the pain in Jack's voice. He was independent, but he had feelings, and right now his heart was breaking. And it hurt.

Jack had a very tough choice to make. Was he really pushed into the decision, like he said? What would you have done given that same ultimatum? An ultimatum is defined as "a final proposition or demand; especially one whose rejection will end negotiations and cause a resort to force or other direct action."

Jack's father had given him only two choices: stop dating Vanessa or leave the family. No one is happy when compromises end and ultimatums are set. Jack's father may have thought he won because he had the final say, but his relationship with his son is falling apart because of his own hatred of another race. Is Jack's father really in control, or is racism controlling him?

Jack may have thought he won by standing up to his father. But he is losing his father.

He did have Vanessa. Her conscience wouldn't let her agree to the decision unless Jack promised to continue to make efforts to repair his relationship with his father. But how long would that take? They were both frightened of the uncertainty they had suddenly been thrown into.

Vanessa asked if there was any other solution. Most schools, including universities, have counselors on campus.

Their job is to help students deal with problems that may be interfering with their education process. The problem could revolve around academics or problems at home. The counseling is usually free and always confidential.

Another resource outside of school is a person who specializes in family issues. Family therapists or family psychologists bring families together to talk things out rationally. They don't tell families what they should do, and they can mediate and facilitate the discussion: What are the parents really uncomfortable about? What do they think will reflect on their family? Parents may also go through this line of questions with themselves after they have objected to the relationship. They may be trying to get a handle on their reaction as well: What's really bothering me? What am I afraid of? Can I get beyond the skin color? Do I really care about the neighbors? Is this person no good for my son or daughter—or no good for me? These are some of the questions parents have to face.

What if Jack and his father had taken the time to let their tempers cool off before things got out of hand like they did? People often count to ten (or 100, depending on the severity) before reacting to a situation. When emotions take over quickly, poor judgments are made, and things are said that are later regretted.

After tempers had cooled off, Jack and his father could have sat down for a meeting. They could have each prepared a list of questions or concerns to discuss. That may sound like something only a perfect television family would do, but it's a more rational approach than ultimatums made in the heat of the moment.

But none of this happened. Instead, Jack and his father reacted without much thought but plenty of emotion. Jack convinced himself that everything would work out okay if he and Vanessa did it together. They both had to be willing and committed. Otherwise, the decision would have left him alone with his principles.

Many interracial couples have had their love unfairly tested in this way. What Jack said about his father bringing them closer together has been true for others. Family members have the unique power to push the fast-forward button on interracial relationships and give them meaning that they might never have had. A three-month relationship can turn overnight into a real-life Romeo and Juliet story. When this happens, a couple will quickly see if their relationship was destined to survive.

Successful couples rely on self-esteem, independence, and strong will, in addition to their true feelings, when dealing with pressures from the outside. You may find all of this overwhelming. Can you handle the pressure? Is it worth it? Can the relationship wait?

What happened to the real Jack and Vanessa? Jack's mother and grandmother made tearful weekly calls begging Jack to change his mind. He stood his ground: His father would not control his life. His father refused to open the lines of communication. Vanessa and Jack's relationship grew stronger. His friends on the rugby team continued to tease him about his relationship with a black girl. When it looked as if Jack had become serious about Vanessa, he lost a few friends. His true close friends were initially hesitant, but eventually they embraced him and Vanessa.

Vanessa's roommate never took a liking to Jack but tolerated him when he came by. Jack tried to get her to like him, but she stood her ground that blacks and whites shouldn't mix.

Jack and Vanessa became a regular couple around campus. A few stares and comments now and then reminded them that they were of different races.

Jack's family never changed their minds. Six months went by, and Jack had barely spoken three words to his father. His grandfather was just as stubborn.

Things begin to change when Jack's father died in a plane crash. Jack depended more and more on Vanessa, questioning her every move that didn't involve him. Vanessa had become not only his family, but his life. He constantly reminded her that he had given up his family for her. The guilt kept her from breaking up with him.

After nearly eighteen months, however, she ended the relationship. It was one of the most difficult decisions she had ever made. The pressure and the circumstances of their relationship had become too overwhelming. She felt like Jack's love for her had turned into an unhealthy, possessive love. She could no longer be all he needed her to be.

Today, Vanessa feels that the ultimatum Jack's father gave to him forced their relationship to become more serious than they were ready for. She believes that if the outside pressures from family, friends, and society had not been so large, their relationship would have had a chance to be what it was—two people who had fallen in love during the first snowfall.

Ultimatums create no-win situations for everyone involved. Eventually, the damage can be repaired if all of the participants are willing to put in the time and effort needed to deal with the problems. Family reactions and pressures from friends tug at our hearts. External pressures from society just make us angry.

Friends are important to our well-being, but you should examine your friends' comments closely. If they object to your relationship, are they really looking out for your own good? Or are they more concerned with how your choice reflects on them and affects their own lives? With parents, remember that honest and open communication, respect for each other's differences, and patience all play vital roles in coping with interracial relationships. You may have to take a different approach when dealing with society in general.

CHAPTER 8

Communication Is the Key

E xternal pressures, meaning pressures from strangers, peers, and so-called friends, are a reality for those involved in interracial relationships. These outside pressures can have as much influence and power over the relationship as the couple gives them. They are going to be ruled by either society's expectations or their own convictions.

"There's a difference between intent and the ability to follow through," says a white male who is married to a Japanese American. "People will say they have no problem with dating outside their race. But then if they start getting flak from those close to them, they may have second thoughts."

As you learned in the previous chapter, interracial dating can be tough without the support of family and friends. You risk parental disapproval, hostility from friends and peers, being labeled, and being taunted about motives. It all seems like a high price to pay for love.

Remember, you're likely to experience many positive reactions, too. It is possible you and your mate will be accepted and you will have a happy, healthy relationship. But it's also likely that you'll receive a number of negative reactions, and it's necessary to focus on handling the challenges.

Opinion Polls

Here are the questions again: Can you handle external pressures? Can you handle the variety of opinions you're likely to encounter, such as "Whatever makes you happy," "People should date their own kind," "Is it true what they say about them in bed?" and "Dating across racial lines promotes racial harmony—go for it"?

Opinions run deep. Pressures could be extreme. It's hard for some to handle. According to a survey taken in 1992 by *Seventeen* magazine, 42 percent of readers who responded said they would date someone of another race or go out with someone of another race. Of the 58 percent who said they would not, 64 percent said it was because the dating would lead to problems if it got serious; 62 percent said their parents wouldn't approve; 46 percent said they themselves didn't approve of interracial dating; and 38 percent said they would feel too self-conscious.

This survey reveals that the pressure is a real factor in considering dating outside of one's race. The number of teens who admit they couldn't handle the pressure outweighs the number who find interracial dating acceptable. But this is just one survey.

Often people will offer their opinion without your asking. And that opinion may come in one of two forms: verbal or nonverbal. Sometimes it may be a combination of both.

Verbal opinions are given in words communicated to you, overheard by you, or relayed to you by someone else. Stares, finger pointing, refusal of service or bad service, handshakes, hugs, and fist fights are few examples of non-verbal communication.

Where cultural or religious differences are present, refusal of entrance and rejection are also examples of non-verbal communication.

For example, one black woman and her white husband were asked to leave a Kwanzaa event sponsored by a church. "While the presenters of the ceremony were describing Umoja (unity), a lady said to me, 'Excuse me, can you tell your friend to leave? You can stay, but he doesn't belong here.' I refused. After she left, someone else came up, followed by another person, and finally one man who asked us to step outside—if you know what I mean. That was enough for me. I was scared for our safety and shaken up emotionally."

Heather and Shawn have experienced the same sort of discrimination.

"I won't go out to the Jockey Club with Shawn," Heather says. "There's always someone in the crowd that's going to say something." It is a predominately black nightclub. Heather says she feels uncomfortable mainly because of the reactions and stares from black women.

Depending on the area you live in, it may be wiser—and safer—to make choices about the places you should go together.

So what do you do when confronted with opposition about your dating choice? Most agree that it is wiser and more mature to simply ignore the comment than risk starting a fight. But sometimes verbal confrontations cannot be avoided, especially when they come from peers, relatives or acquaintances.

If you choose to defend your relationship, always accentuate the positives and the beauty of the relationship. Talking in terms of genuine feelings and personal happiness shames most critics into silence. You can make them see that *they* have the problem.

On the positive side, interracial couples hear comments like, "You guys make a cute couple," "Your boyfriend is so gorgeous, I wish I had the nerve to date someone outside of my race," or "It's beautiful to see our races finally getting along."

Interracial couples often have friends who are involved in mixed relationships as well. They share a unique bond, knowing the frustrations and pressures society places on those who don't follow normal dating patterns. They share their experiences and laugh about their encounters. It's another good way of coping, they say.

You make new friends as well. Heather, a physical trainer, has found that when people of color—both men and women—find out she's married to a black man, they are more accepting of her.

Many couples say they love the attention they get from strangers. It gives strangers an opportunity to see a healthy, happy couple. It may remove some of their negative thinking and stereotyping as well. Couples say it's important to remember that not all stares or reactions are negative.

External pressures can be positive in the sense that they lead you and your partner to self-examination. How ready are you to be part of a couple? Teenagers usually want a trouble-free, fun-filled relationship. However, a fun-filled experience doesn't always come right away for any couple—especially interracial couples.

Open and Honest Communication

Psychologists have found that interracial couples date longer and stay married longer than same-race couples. Why? Couples who have learned to cope with interracial dating say that outside pressures will bring you closer, strengthen your relationship, and give you a better appreciation of your love.

You can take some key steps if you are dating interracially and have decided that your relationship is ready to move to a more serious stage.

Communication is essential. Discuss your feelings when you encounter stereotypes against mixed couples in books, on television, or in your daily lives at school or work. Try to support each other while reaffirming your commitment, despite the social pressures against you. If you only associate with real friends who accept your relationship, it will help ease other outside pressures or difficulties.

Look for other couples who are in interracial relationships and who share your experiences. You can even chat with teenagers and adults from around the world through the Internet. It's easy. Just type in the word "**interracial dating**" and do a search. One of the sites that will come up belongs to the International Interracial Association. Their address is listed in the back of this book, along with others.

Another site belongs to *Interrace Magazine*. It's a national magazine for interracial couples, families, singles, and multiracial people. *Interrace Magazine* includes articles on interracial family living, transracial adoption, dating, multiracial identity, raising biracial or multiracial children, and race relations in general.

Understanding, patience, and compromising are three other key elements to success. Although interracial couples are just couples like everyone else, they face unique challenges. They may have to become accustomed to a little more than the funny way a boyfriend or girlfriend chews food.

A partner from a different culture may have to be patient with an American mate. In turn, the American may have to accept that some customs and traditions may not include him or her.

A partner who speaks another language may have to be patient with a mate who chooses not to learn or has difficulty grasping the language. Does the mate have to learn the language? No, but he or she may feel more comfortable in gatherings where the language is spoken. Otherwise, he or she may feel left out. If one person is not willing to learn, or if the other is not willing to include the other in the conversation, resentment could build up and eventually destroy the relationship.

Your interracial relationship will not be all roses. You may experience small communication breakdowns because you and your partner are looking at the world through different cultural eyes. Nonetheless, the learning process that happens throughout the course of the relationship can be a wonderful, shared experience that brings you closer together emotionally.

Outside and parental pressures usually taper off as the newness of the relationship wears off. Then it's usually just the ordinary ups and downs of any dating relationship. That's when you know if your relationship is based on real feelings or just on the excitement of going against the norm or against your parents' wishes.

Those who last through the casual or curious stage of interracial or cross-cultural dating and are serious about continuing the relationship should seek books on dating in general. A reading list at the end of this book can help you get started. Advice on maintaining a relationship is also readily available in many magazines, such as *Seventeen*, *Teen*, *YM*, and *Glamour.*

Here are ten ways one expert says you can keep love alive; they appeared in *Glamour* magazine. These guidelines are helpful for any relationship, interracial or not:

- Love yourself first: If you hope to build something strong, it helps to start with the best possible material—you;
- Be prepared for an emotional rollercoaster ride: All of a sudden you will realize that the person you've fallen in love with is just another human being. He or she has faults and makes mistakes. Once you take off the rose-colored spectacles, reality will shine through. Make sure you're ready for it;
- Learn to listen: The more you learn about your mate, the easier it is to communicate;
- Learn to talk: It's better to say, "What you did made me angry and I need to talk about it," than to hold your anger inside;
- Give the relationship some room: Once the two of you are certain of your compatibility—physical, emotional, and intellectual—it's time for you to step back and see how well the relationship grows on its own, without constant prompting from each other;
- Treasure your private time together: Both of you lead busy, active lives, but the success of your

relationship depends upon your ability to make time for each other;

- Be tolerant: Under no circumstances should you expect your mate to change in order to meet your specifications. As far as you're concerned, your mate's individuality, and that includes faults, should be his or her most appealing quality;
- Don't forget romance: Find some way to say, "I care about you." You don't always have to say it with words;
- Be supportive: No matter what bad hand your mate is being dealt, it's important that you be there to remind them that the game isn't over; and finally;
- Keep your sense of humor: Your ability to see the lighter side of things, even when times get rough, can mean the difference between the success or failure of your relationship.

Are those things race-oriented or simply human-oriented? That's what interracial or cross-cultural couples are: human. Being human is one element that should always be included.

Making choices is often difficult. Sometimes it is not clear whether a decision is the right one. As you grow older and gain more experience and knowledge, more choices will come your way. Some of those choices will be more difficult than deciding whether or not to date someone of another race or culture.

A poem by Robert Frost talks about choices. In a "A Road Not Taken," the speaker is a traveler who comes to a fork in the road. One road looks like many have traveled it; the other looks as if few have headed that way. He examines his choices because he knows he'll never be at the same fork in the road again.

Here's what he finally decided:

"Two roads diverged in a wood, and I—
I took the one less traveled by,
And that has made all the difference."

Many more teenagers and adults will face similar forks in the road. Listed at the end of this book are a few organizations that are concerned with interracial and cross-cultural matters.

Part of coping with anything that challenges us is learning how to reach out to others for support. You'll find that there are many organizations for interracial couples. They'll tell you where to go for help and how to find the answers you need.

Interracial dating is a personal choice. The willingness to go against what's considered "normal" may bring about overwhelming pressures. Despite the reactions, fears, and concerns from others and the ignorance and prejudices you'll encounter, the decision is ultimately yours.

Glossary

affirmative action Policies designed to actively encourage the hiring and promotion of minorities and women.

apartheid An official policy of racial segregation practiced in the Republic of South Africa until the early 1990s.

assimilate To absorb and incorporate; to become similar.

bias Impartial judgment or preference.

biracial Made up of two races.

boycott To avoid buying something or participating in something as an act of protest.

compromise A settlement in which both parties make some concessions in order to reach a solution.

culture Behavior patterns, beliefs, and other shared characteristics of a community or people.

customs Common traditions and practices that have usually been practiced for many generations.

derogatory Insulting.

discrimination An action based on prejudice.

disparaging Belittling; degrading.

diversity Difference; variety.

epithet An abusive word or phrase used to describe a person.

ethnic Pertaining to a religious, racial, national, or cultural group.

ethnocentrism A belief that one's own ethnic group is superior to others.

extermination Complete destruction.

felony A crime such as a rape, burglary, or murder; punished more seriously than a misdemeanor.

happenstance A chance occurrence.

heritage Something passed on through the generations; a legacy or tradition.

homophobic Fear of homosexuality.

ignorance A lack of knowledge.

interracial Between races.

intraracism Racism among members of the same race.

lynching An illegal execution, especially by hanging.

mainstream The ideas or influences followed by most of the members of a society.

motive An impulse that drives one to commit a certain action.

multiethnic Consisting of many ethnic groups.

norm A standard or pattern that is considered typical for members of a certain group.

oppression The state of being dominated by an unjust force or authority.

pathological Exhibiting disordered behavior.

prejudice An opinion or judgment formed beforehand, without examination of the facts.

provocative Exciting, stimulating.

racism The idea that one's own race is superior and other races are inferior.

scapegoat A person or group that is unfairly blamed for wrong caused by others.

segregation Separation of different races.

separatism A belief that different races should not associate with each other.

sexual orientation Sexual identity: heterosexuality, homo-sexuality, or bisexuality, for example.

Skinhead A person, usually a white male, who belongs to any various, sometimes violent youth gangs whose members have close-shaven hair and often promote white-supremacist beliefs.

slavery A practice in which human beings were bought and sold, and lived with and worked for the "master" who owned them. In the United States, Africans were brought from Africa as slaves in colonial times and continued to be enslaved until after the Civil War.

stereotype   An oversimplified but commonly held opinion or belief.

taboo   A belief prohibiting something because it violates society's religious or moral values.

trait   A distinguishing feature or quality.

ultimatum   A statement in an argument or negotiation in which one party threatens that the other party will suffer consequences if the first party's terms are not accepted.

values   Principles or qualities considered desirable.

Where to Go for Help

Association for Multicultural Counseling and Development
5999 Stevenson Avenue
Alexandria, VA 22304

Association of MultiEthnic Americans
P.O. Box 191726
San Francisco, CA 94119-1726

Interracial Family Circle
P.O. Box 53290
Washington, DC 20009

Interracial Intercultural Pride (I-Pride)
P.O. Box 191752
San Francisco, CA 94119-1752

Interrace Magazine
P.O. Box 12048
Atlanta, GA 30355
(404) 350-7877

Interrace: The Source for Interracial Living
P.O. Box 15566
Beverly Hills, CA 90209

Society for Interracial Families Newsletter
23399 Evergreen
Suite 2222
Southfield, MI 48075

WEB SITES

http://icg.resnet.upenn.edu/~konrad/iia.html
The homepage for the Interracial International Association, promoting interracial and intercultural harmony worldwide.

http://starcreations.com/idc/idc-link.htm
The homepage for the Inter-cultural Dating club.

http://www.eden.com/~crusader/irhaven.html
The homepage for interracial couples, individuals and their families.

For Further Reading

Almonte, Paul, and Desmond, Theresa. *The Facts About Inter-racial Marriage*. New York: Crestwood House, 1992.

Bode, Janet. *Different Worlds: Interracial and Cross-Cultural Dating*. New York: Franklin Watts, 1989.

Funderburg, Lisa. *Black, White, Other: Biracial Americans Talk About Race and Identity*. New York: William Morrow and Co., 1994.

Gay, Kathryn. *The Rainbow Effect: Interracial Families*. New York: Franklin Watts, 1987.

———. *I Am Who I Am: Speaking Out About Multiracial Identity*. New York: Franklin Watts, 1995.

Landau, Elaine. *Interracial Dating*. New York: Silver Burdett Press, 1993.

Mathabane, Gail, and Mathabane, Mark. *Love in Black and White: The Triumph of Love Over Prejudice and Taboo*. New York: HarperCollins, 1992.

Nash, Renea. *Coping as a Biracial/Biethnic Teen*. New York: The Rosen Publishing Group, 1995.

Tizard Barbara. *Black, White, or Mixed Race?: Race and Racism in the Lives of Young People of Mixed Parentage*. New York: Routledge, 1993.

Index